Quick Study

Science

PEARSON
Scott
Foresman

Editorial Offices: Glenview, Illinois • Parsippany, New Jersey • New York, New York
Sales Offices: Needham, Massachusetts • Duluth, Georgia • Glenview, Illinois
Coppell, Texas • Sacramento, California • Mesa, Arizona

www.sfsuccessnet.com

Series Authors

Dr. Timothy Cooney
Professor of Earth Science and Science Education
University of Northern Iowa (UNI)
Cedar Falls, Iowa

Dr. Jim Cummins
Professor
Department of Curriculum,
Teaching, and Learning
The University of Toronto
Toronto, Canada

Dr. James Flood
Distinguished Professor of Literacy and Language
School of Teacher Education
San Diego State University
San Diego, California

Barbara Kay Foots, M.Ed.
Science Education Consultant
Houston, Texas

Dr. M. Jenice Goldston
Associate Professor of Science Education
Department of Elementary Education
Programs
University of Alabama
Tuscaloosa, Alabama

Dr. Shirley Gholston Key
Associate Professor of Science Education
Instruction and Curriculum Leadership
Department
College of Education
University of Memphis
Memphis, Tennessee

Dr. Diane Lapp
Distinguished Professor of Reading and Language Arts in Teacher Education
San Diego State University
San Diego, California

Sheryl A. Mercier
Classroom Teacher
Dunlap Elementary School
Dunlap, California

Dr. Karen L. Ostlund
UTeach, College of Natural Sciences
The University of Texas at Austin
Austin, Texas

Dr. Nancy Romance
Professor of Science Education & Principal Investigator
NSF/IERI Science IDEAS Project
Charles E. Schmidt College of Science
Florida Atlantic University
Boca Raton, Florida

Dr. William Tate
Chair and Professor of Education and Applied Statistics
Department of Education
Washington University
St. Louis, Missouri

Dr. Kathryn C. Thornton
Professor
School of Engineering and Applied
Science
University of Virginia
Charlottesville, Virginia

Dr. Leon Ukens
Professor of Science Education
Department of Physics, Astronomy,
and Geosciences
Towson University
Towson, Maryland

Steve Weinberg
Consultant
Connecticut Center for Advanced
Technology
East Hartford, Connecticut

Consulting Author

Dr. Michael P. Klentschy
Superintendent
El Centro Elementary School District
El Centro, California

Unit C
Physical Science

Unit D
Space and Technology

Lesson 1: Why do we classify?

Vocabulary

classify to put things into groups

kingdom the highest or most general group of organisms

phylum the second level of classification below the level of kingdom

class the level of classification below phylum

species the lowest level of classification

Lewis and Clark's Mission of Discovery

Meriwether Lewis and William Clark were explorers. They looked for a route between the Atlantic and Pacific Oceans. Lewis and Clark described and collected samples of plants and animals that lived in the West. Later, biologists used these samples to **classify** organisms. They put organisms into groups. To group organisms, biologists studied each organism carefully. Then they compared the new information with plants and animals they had already studied. They put organisms that were similar in one group. They put plants or animals that were different in new groups.

Reasons to Classify

A classification system puts organisms into groups. In this system, each organism has just one name. This makes it easier for scientists to organize information. An organism's group tells scientists a lot about that organism. For example, most organisms that are classified as a plant need sunlight to live. If scientists didn't have a classification system, they might call one organism by different names. Or they might give the same name to more than one organism.

Classification Systems

The classification system scientists use today has changed over many years. It is always changing. For example, scientists in the past divided organisms into two **kingdoms**—the plant and animal kingdoms. Today, there are six kingdoms: plant, animal, archaebacteria, eubacteria, protists, and fungi. Scientists put similar organisms into groups. Each group is called a **phylum.** A phylum is a group below the level of kingdom. Scientists compare and contrast the organisms in each kingdom. Then they separate organisms in each phylum into smaller groups called **classes.** Classes are below the level of phylum. Scientists divide each level of organisms into smaller and smaller levels, called order, family, and genus. The lowest level is called the **species.**

© Pearson Education, Inc. **5**

Lesson 1 Checkpoint

1. How do scientists classify organisms?

_____

_____

2. Describe one advantage of having a classification system.

_____

_____

3. What kinds of observations did scientists use at first to group organisms into a phylum or class?

_____

_____

Lesson 2: How do we classify vertebrates?

Vocabulary

vertebrate an organism with a backbone

Characteristics of Animals

Animals are made up of more than one cell. They are multicellular. Animals like bears are made of trillions of cells. Animals cannot make their own food. They must eat other organisms. Animals can move on their own during part or all of their lives.

Vertebrate Animals

Animals like bison and sheep have backbones. Animals with backbones are **vertebrates.** Backbones protect nerves that go to the brain. Five classes of vertebrates are mammals, reptiles, birds, amphibians, and fish.

Mammals

All mammals breathe air with lungs. Most mammals have hair or fur all over their bodies. Mammals are warm-blooded. They keep their body temperature almost the same all the time. Mammals usually look like their parents at birth. Mothers make milk for their babies.

Reptiles

Reptiles have tough, dry skin with scales. Reptiles are cold-blooded. Their blood temperature changes. Snakes, lizards, and turtles are reptiles. Reptiles hatch from eggs. They can look for food right after birth.

Birds

Birds are warm-blooded vertebrates. Their wings have feathers that help them fly. Some birds have wings shaped like an airplane's wings. The front edge of their wing is wide. The top of the wing curves back to a thin edge. Not all birds can fly. Baby birds hatch from eggs. Baby birds are fed by their parents.

Amphibians

Frogs, toads, and salamanders are amphibians. Amphibians are cold-blooded. They have soft, moist skin. Their skin can absorb water and oxygen. All amphibians hatch from eggs. When they are young, most of them are tadpoles. At first, they breathe using gills. As they get older, they grow legs and their tails get shorter. They stop breathing with gills and live on land. Grown frogs look very different from when they were young. No other vertebrates change this much in their lifetime.

Fish

Fish are vertebrates. They live in water. Fish breathe through gills found on each side of the head. Most fish have scales. Fish also have a slimy coating that helps water flow past them. Fish hatch from soft eggs. They can feed themselves right away.

Discovery of Dinosaur Fossils

In the early 1800s, scientists began to classify ancient animal bones. These bones came from species that were no longer living. Scientists compared these bones to the bones of living animals. Scientists believed that the ancient bones came from animals like huge lizards. They called these animals *dinosaurs.*

Comparing Dinosaurs to Today's Animals

Dinosaurs had backbones and scales like today's lizards. Many walked on four legs. They had a heart similar to a bird's or mammal's heart. Some dinosaurs even had feathers!

Lesson 2 Checkpoint

1. What are 3 of the features that make animals different from other organisms?

_____

_____

2. ⊙ **Compare and Contrast** How would you compare and contrast a squirrel and a bear?

_____

_____

_____

3. How are some bird wings like airplane wings?

_____

_____

4. In addition to them both being vertebrate animals, how else are amphibians and fish similar?

_____

_____

5. ⊙ **Compare and Contrast** mammals and fish.

_____

_____

6. Name the classes of living vertebrates discussed in the lesson. Give one example from each class.

_____

_____

_____

_____

7. What characteristics do dinosaurs and today's animals share?

_____

_____

Lesson 3: How do we classify invertebrates?

Vocabulary

invertebrates animals without backbones

Animals Without Backbones

Most animals do not have backbones. They are invertebrates. Some **invertebrates** are so small that you cannot see them. Giant squids are the largest invertebrates. They can stretch across a basketball court. Some other invertebrates are mollusks, worms, cnidarians, and arthropods.

Mollusks

The body of a mollusk is soft. It does not have bones. Some mollusks have a hard outer shell that protects them from being eaten. This phylum includes snails, slugs, clams, and squids. Some mollusks get oxygen by using gills. Others absorb oxygen through their skin.

Worms

There are many kinds of worms. Flatworms are very flat and thin. They live in wet or damp places. Roundworms live in water or on land. The earthworm is a segmented worm. This means that its body is made of different pieces. Some worms are too small to see without a microscope. Others are huge. The largest earthworm caught was about 7 meters (23 feet) long.

Cnidaria

Jellyfish belong to the Cnidaria phylum. Jellyfish hatch from eggs. A young jellyfish, or larva, swims for days or weeks before attaching to a new place. It attaches itself to the ocean floor. After it does this, it is called a polyp. The polyp grows. Pieces of it fall off, or bud, to form new jellyfish.

Arthropods

The Arthropod phylum is the largest phylum of animals. Arthropods are invertebrates. Insects, lobsters, and spiders are all arthropods. Arthropods have legs with joints. They also have bodies that are divided into separate parts.

Different arthropods breathe in different ways. Lobsters have gills. Grasshoppers have tubes that carry air through their body. Spiders breathe with book lungs.

Arthropods like butterflies, moths, and houseflies have life cycles that include big changes. This kind of life cycle is called complete metamorphosis. Other arthropods, like grasshoppers, hatch from eggs. They look like adults when they hatch. This life cycle is called incomplete metamorphosis.

Identifying Organisms

A dichotomous key is used to identify organisms. Dichotomous keys ask questions about unknown organisms. By following the arrows to the correct answers, you can find out what the unknown organism is. (Look at page 21 in your textbook.) Some keys can only identify trees. Other keys can identify birds. Each key helps identify certain organisms.

© Pearson Education, Inc. **5**

Lesson 3 Checkpoint

1. List at least 3 different invertebrates. How are they alike?

_____

_____

_____

2. ⊙ **Compare and Contrast** How are worms and clams alike? How are they different?

_____

_____

_____

3. Choose two animals on page 21 of your textbook and use the key to classify and identify them.

_____

_____

_____

_____

4. Choose 5 or 6 objects from the classroom. Create a dichotomous key with which you could identify them.

Lesson 4: How are other organisms classified?

Qualities of Plants

Plants are different from animals. Plants use sunlight, water, and carbon dioxide to make their own food. Plants have roots and leaves. Many plants are vascular. This means they have special tubes that carry food and water to all parts of the plant. Four common types of plant phyla are mosses, ferns, conifers, and flowering plants.

Mosses

Mosses grow on trees or in shallow streams. A single moss plant is very small. Mosses are not vascular. Mosses have tiny parts that look like leaves. They don't have flowers or seeds.

Ferns

Most ferns have leaves that look like feathers. Ferns are vascular. Vascular plants can grow larger than nonvascular plants. This is because vascular plants have tubes that carry food to parts of the plant that are high off the ground. Mosses and ferns use spores to reproduce. Spores are tiny cells that can grow into plants.

Conifers

Pine, fir, and spruce trees are all conifers. Many conifers have special leaves called needles. Conifers are vascular plants. They reproduce using cones and seeds.

Flowering Plants

There are about 230,000 species of flowering plants. All flowering plants are vascular. These plants use their flowers' seeds to reproduce. Mosses, ferns, and conifers don't produce flowers.

Neither Plant nor Animal

Many organisms do not belong in either the plant or animal kingdoms. Some of these organisms can move on their own like animals, but they make their own food like plants. Some organisms are made of one cell. These can only be seen through a microscope. Others are single cells that live together in groups. Some of these microscopic organisms can cause disease. Others can be helpful. Like plants and animals, all these organisms need food, water, and a way to remove waste. Many also need carbon dioxide or oxygen.

Debates in Classifying

The classification system has changed over the years. This is because scientists find new organisms. Biologists don't always agree on how many kingdoms there should be. There have been classification systems with four, five, or more kingdoms. One classification system used today has six kingdoms. These kingdoms are plants, animals, fungi, protists, eubacteria, and archaebacteria.

Biologists may disagree on how to classify some new organisms. This happens when a new organism is like organisms in two different groups.

Fungi, such as mushrooms, are not plants. They cannot make their own food. Mushrooms absorb food from the material they grow on. Yeast are single-celled fungi. To reproduce, each cell divides into two cells.

Most protists are single cells. Protists such as algae are food for many animals. Some protists live in the digestive systems of some animals, like termites and cows. They help these animals digest plants they eat. These animals would die without protists.

Eubacteria are single cells. They can have many different shapes. Some have tails that move them through water.

Archaebacteria are single cells. They can survive in environments that are deadly for most other organisms. They can live in hot acid springs or in very salty water.

© Pearson Education, Inc. 5

Lesson 4 Checkpoint

1. How would you classify a plant that has seeds, is vascular, and has needle-like leaves?

_____

2. How do protists help some animals?

_____

_____

_____

3. How are the needs of single-celled organisms similar to the needs of plants or animals?

_____

_____

4. Why has the classification system changed over the years?

_____

_____

_____

5. 🎯 **Compare and Contrast** Compare the fungi and protist kingdoms.

_____

_____

_____

Lesson 1: What is inside a cell?

Vocabulary

cell membrane surrounds a cell, holding the parts of the cell together; allows certain materials to enter the cell and waste products to exit

nucleus contains chromosomes that control how the body grows and changes

cytoplasm all the contents of the cell outside the nucleus

vacuole store and break down materials; in plants they may store water

cell wall tough material surrounding the cell membrane in plant cells that provides support and protection

chloroplast contains a green substance that uses the energy in sunlight to turn water and carbon dioxide into oxygen and sugar

Cells and Their Functions

Cells are the most basic unit of living things. They are the smallest living part of an organism. A single cell is so tiny that you need a microscope to see it. Organisms can be made of only one cell. Organisms made of many cells are called multicellular. Cells have the same needs as you do. They need food. Cells must also get rid of waste. Cells also need energy. Cells use energy to grow, move, and to make new cells. Cells get energy from respiration. Respiration is the mixing of oxygen and food to make energy.

The Parts of Cells

All cells have parts. Some parts are like parts in your body. The **cell membrane** is like your skin. It holds the cell together. The cell membrane lets some materials, such as water, sugar and oxygen, enter the cell. The cell membrane also lets waste products leave the cell. The cell's **nucleus** contains chromosomes. Chromosomes tell the body how to grow and change. Chromosomes are made of a chemical called DNA. Every chromosome has small sections called genes. Almost every cell in your body has the same set of genes.

Cytoplasm is the material between the cell membrane and the nucleus. Mitochondria mix oxygen and food to make energy. **Vacuoles** act like a stomach. They store food and break down waste.

Plant Cells

Plant cells have the same parts as animal cells. They also have parts that animal cells don't have. Plant cells have a **cell wall** and **chloroplasts.** A cell wall surrounds the cell membrane. It gives the cell extra support and protection. Chloroplasts give plants their green color. They turn water and carbon dioxide into oxygen and sugar. Plant cells use oxygen and sugar for respiration.

The Size of Cells

Like most things, cells have a limit to how big or small they can be. They cannot be too small or too large. If they are too small, they will not have room for all their parts. If they are too big, oxygen and other materials cannot reach the middle of the cell quickly. This would cause the cell to die.

Lesson 1 Checkpoint

1. What is the most basic unit of living things?

_____

_____

2. 🎯 **Draw Conclusions** Suppose you saw a small organism move across your desk. Would you infer that this organism was multicellular or a single cell?

_____

_____

3. Describe why cells have limits as to how big or small they can be.

_____

_____

_____

_____

4. List five parts of all cells and their jobs.

_____

_____

_____

_____

_____

Lesson 2: How do cells work together?

Vocabulary

tissue a group of the same kind of cells working together doing the same job

organ a grouping of different tissues combined together into one structure to perform a main job in the body

Types of Cells and Their Work

There are about 200 different kinds of cells in your body. Cells have different jobs. A cell's shape helps the cell do its job.

Branching Cells

Nerves cells carry signals between the brain and the rest of the body. Nerve cells look like tree branches. These branching shapes connect many parts of the body. This helps signals reach the brain quickly.

Flat Cells

Flat cells join together to cover a surface. Your skin has many layers of flat cells. This makes your skin strong. Flat cells are also on the inside of your mouth and stomach.

Round Cells

Red blood cells move through blood vessels easily because they are smooth. Red blood cells look like small discs. Their shape helps them pick up oxygen and carry it to all the cells in your body.

Special Cell Structure

Cells have different structures. For example, muscle cells have long thread-like fibers. Cells in your ears and lungs have structures like hair. In the lungs, these structures are called cilia. They sweep dirt and germs out of your airways.

Cells Form Tissues

Cells usually don't work by themselves. They often work in **tissues.** Tissues are like teams of cells that work together. Cells in tissues do the same job. Muscle tissue is made of muscle cells grouped together. Bone cells grouped together make up bone tissue. Nerve cells grouped together make up nerve tissue.

Tissues Form Organs

Tissues join together to make **organs.** Your heart, eyes, ears, and stomach are organs. Your body's largest organ is your skin.

Organs have jobs. Hair is a tissue in the organ of your skin. It protects your skin. It holds warm air next to your body. Sweat glands are tissues in your skin. They make sweat. Sweat helps cool your skin. Sweat also carries waste products from the cells.

Plants have organs too. Stems, roots, leaves, and flowers are all plant organs.

Skin Cell Tissue

Skin cells form in many layers. New cells are made in the bottom layers. They push older cells away from any blood supply. Older cells are dead when they reach the outside surface of the skin. The dead cells fall off your body.

Other Tissues in the Skin

Skin has many tissues. They work together to do many jobs. Skin protects your insides. Skin keeps out germs. Skin doesn't let too much water leave your body. Nerve tissue in your skin helps you sense touch and temperature. Blood vessels carry food and oxygen to cells. Oil glands keep your skin soft. When you are cold, muscle tissue makes the hair on your skin stand up. The hairs trap warm air next to the skin and keeps the skin warm.

Lesson 2 Checkpoint

1. What are cilia and what do they do?

_____

_____

_____

_____

2. How does a nerve cell's shape and structure help it do its job?

_____

_____

_____

_____

3. How is a tissue like a team?

_____

_____

4. **Draw Conclusions** Why is it an advantage to have dead cells on the surface of the skin?

_____

_____

_____

_____

Lesson 3: How do organs work together?

Vocabulary

organ system a group of organs and tissues that work together to carry out a life process

Organ Systems

Cells work together in tissues. Tissues work together in organs. Organs work together as part of an **organ system.** For example, the mouth, stomach, intestines, and other organs work together to digest food.

Bones Form a System

Each bone is an organ. There are about 200 bones in the skeletal system. This organ system gives your body support. The skeletal system also protects important organs. The skull is made of bones that protect your brain. The rib cage is made of bones that protect your lungs and heart.

Muscles Work as a System

Muscles are organs. They work together to move your body. There are about 640 muscles that you control. When you run, your brain tells your muscles how to work together. Other muscles work by themselves. When you shiver, muscles work to warm the body. You do not have to think about shivering. It happens without your thinking about it.

Organ Systems Work Together

The muscle and skeletal systems work together to move your body. Muscles work in pairs to move bones.

Try this. Hold your arm out straight in front of you. Bend your elbow. The muscle on the bottom of your arm relaxes. The muscle on top of your upper arm tightens. This pulls on the bone of your upper arm and makes your elbow bend. The opposite happens when you stretch your arm. The bottom of your upper arm tightens. The top of your arm relaxes.

Other Systems Work Together

Your organ systems work together too. For example, your nervous system controls how your muscles move bones. Nerves carry signals from your brain and spinal cord to your muscles. Without nerves, your muscles would never move.

Some organs work for more than one organ system. For example, muscles don't just work with bones. Muscles in your heart push blood through your blood vessels.

5

Quick Study

Lesson 3 Checkpoint

1. How many bones make up the skeletal system?

_____

2. List some organ systems and describe their jobs.

_____

_____

3. How do muscles work in pairs to move a bone?

_____

_____

_____

Lesson 1: What is the circulatory system?

Vocabulary

artery a type of blood vessel that carries blood away from the heart to other parts of the body

capillary the thinnest artery

vein a type of blood vessel that carries blood from the cells back to the heart

valve an opening that allows blood to flow in one direction but stops it from flowing in the other direction

The Body's Transportation System

The circulatory system brings food and oxygen to every cell in your body. It also takes away cell waste. The heart, blood, and blood vessels are part of the circulatory system. Blood vessels are tubes that carry blood through the body.

Functions of the Blood

Your blood has many parts. Each part has a different job. Plasma in your blood brings food and water to your cells. Plasma also takes away waste and moves chemicals from one part of the body to another.

Red blood cells in your blood carry oxygen to cells in the body. Your cells need oxygen to get energy from food.

White blood cells protect your body against germs and harmful things. Your body makes more white blood cells when it needs to fight infection. Some white blood cells carry chemicals that kill germs. Other white blood cells wrap around the germ and break it down.

Platelets are pieces of cells that float in the blood. Platelets stop bleeding by sticking together near the edges of a cut.

Arteries, Capillaries, and Veins

The circulatory system has three kinds of blood vessels. **Arteries** carry blood away from the heart to other parts of your body. Almost all arteries carry blood with lots of oxygen. Arteries branch many times into smaller and smaller tubes.

Capillaries are the smallest blood vessels. Oxygen from your blood passes through the walls to your cells. Carbon dioxide and other wastes move from cells into capillaries. Capillaries carry blood into veins. **Veins** are blood vessels that bring blood from cells back to the heart. Veins have valves. **Valves** are flaps that keep blood flowing in one direction.

Parts of the Heart

The heart pumps blood through the circulatory system. The heart has two sides. Each side has two parts. The upper part of each side is called an atrium. The lower part is called a ventricle.

Blood flows through all four parts of the heart. Veins carry blood into the right atrium. This blood carries waste and carbon dioxide from cells. The right atrium pushes the blood into the right ventricle. Next, the right ventricle pumps the blood into an artery that goes to the lungs. The blood gets oxygen in the lungs. Then the blood flows into the left atrium. The left atrium pushes blood into the left ventricle. The left ventricle pumps blood with oxygen into your arteries. This blood is sent to body cells.

© Pearson Education, Inc. 5

Lesson 1 Checkpoint

1. What is the job of the circulatory system?

_____

_____

2. What is the function of white blood cells?

_____

_____

3. How are the jobs of a vein and an artery the same? How are they different?

_____

_____

4. Identify common diseases of the circulatory system.

_____

_____

5. What is the job of your heart's left atrium?

_____

_____

Lesson 2: What is the respiratory system?

Vocabulary

mucus a sticky, thick fluid that traps dust, germs, and other things that may be in the air

trachea a tube that carries air from the throat to the lungs

bronchioles tubes that branch out from the bronchi

air sacs tiny thin-walled pouches in the lungs

Parts of the Respiratory System

Your body cells need oxygen. Your cells make another gas called carbon dioxide. Your respiratory system carries these gases in and out of your body. Your respiratory system works when you breathe.

Air enters the respiratory system through the nose or mouth. Then the air goes from the throat into the larynx. The vocal cords are in the larynx. Your vocal cords move when you speak.

Air travels from the larynx into the **trachea.** The trachea carries air to the lungs. The trachea leads to two branches called bronchi that go into the lungs. The bronchi branch into smaller tubes called **bronchioles.**

Air sacs are at the end of each bronchiole. Air sacs are like tiny bags of air. They have very thin walls. Air sacs are where oxygen enters the blood and carbon dioxide leaves the blood.

Mucus coats many parts of the respiratory system. Mucus is a sticky, thick liquid that traps dust and germs.

How You Breathe

Many muscles work together when you breathe. The **diaphragm** tightens and moves down when you breathe in. This makes more space in your chest. Air fills this new space.

The diaphragm loosens when you breathe out. This makes less space in your chest. Air is pushed out and leaves the respiratory system through the mouth or nose.

Respiratory and Circulatory Systems Work Together

How do your cells get the oxygen they need? The respiratory system and the circulatory system work together.

First, the respiratory system brings oxygen from the air into your body. This happens when you breathe in. Air comes into your lungs. It fills your air sacs.

Then the circulatory system starts to work. Blood picks up oxygen from the air sacs. It carries the oxygen to every body cell. Cells produce carbon dioxide when they use oxygen. Blood also carries this waste back to the air sacs. The carbon dioxide leaves your body when you breathe out.

The chart on page 72 in your textbook explains some diseases of the respiratory system. For example, a cold is caused by a virus. Signs of a cold are a runny nose and sneezing. Tuberculosis is caused by bacteria. Signs of tuberculosis are a cough, fever, and shortness of breath. Lung cancer is caused by tobacco and chemicals.

Lesson 2 Checkpoint

1. What is the job of the air sacs?

_____

_____

2. Describe how the respiratory and circulatory systems work together.

_____

_____

_____

3. Identify common diseases of the respiratory system and their causes.

_____

_____

4. 🎯 **Sequence** What is the order of structures that oxygen passes through between your nose and bloodstream?

_____

_____

_____

_____

Lesson 3: What are the digestive and urinary systems?

Vocabulary

esophagus a tube in the throat with rings of muscle that help you to swallow food

Digestive System

How does your body get energy from the food you eat? The digestive system breaks down the food into very small materials. Then the food can enter your cells. The digestive system is made of many organs that help you digest food.

The Mouth and Esophagus

The first step of digestion is chewing. Chewing makes food smaller so you can swallow it. Front teeth help you cut food when you bite. Teeth in the back of the mouth are flatter. They help you crush food. The tongue moves food and helps you swallow. Then the food enters the **esophagus.** Muscles in the esophagus push food into the stomach.

Stomach

There is a muscle at the bottom of your esophagus. This muscle opens when you swallow to let food into the stomach. Then the muscle closes so food cannot move back into the esophagus.

The walls of the stomach can stretch to store food. The stomach produces fluids that help digest food. Strong muscles in the stomach squeeze to mix these fluids with food.

Food is ready to leave the stomach when it becomes a wet paste. The stomach squeezes the food into a long, winding tube called the small intestine. The liver and pancreas are organs that send chemicals to the small intestine. These chemicals help digest food.

The walls of the small intestine are lined with structures called villi. They are shaped like tiny fingers. The villi help the small intestine collect food. Villi have very thin walls. Capillaries are under these walls. Food moves from the villi into the capillaries. Then the blood brings this food to body cells.

Some food cannot be digested. This food waste moves from the small intestine into the large intestine. The large intestine takes water and salts from the waste to make it more solid. Finally, muscles squeeze the waste out of the body.

The Urinary System

Your body cells make waste. They send this waste into the blood. It can make your body sick. The urinary system removes the waste from your blood.

Your kidneys are two organs that remove waste from the blood. Water, salt, and other chemicals also leave the blood when waste is removed. Your body needs some of these materials. The kidneys put the right amount of each material back into your blood.

The kidneys take out some water with the waste. This mix of waste and water is urine. A tube carries the urine from the kidneys to the urinary bladder. A tight muscle sits at the bottom of the bladder. It keeps urine inside the bladder until it leaves the body.

Lesson 3 Checkpoint

1. What is the job of the digestive system?

_____

_____

2. What parts of the structure of the small intestine are specially shaped to help the intestine do its job?

_____

_____

3. Explain how the urinary system regulates the blood.

_____

_____

4. How does the digestive system work together with the circulatory system to keep your body healthy?

_____

_____

Lesson 1: How do leaves help a plant?

Vocabulary

photosynthesis the process that plants and some other organisms use
to make sugar for food

Cells and Tissues in Leaves

Plants make their own food. Most plants have leaves. Most of a plant's food is made in its leaves. Leaves have different layers of cells. Tissues are layers of similar cells. The outside layer of a leaf is called the epidermis tissue. The epidermis is made of flat cells. This layer is like the top layer of your skin. It protects the plant. The inner layer looks like a sponge. It has spaces that air can pass through. Air enters this layer through tiny holes at the bottom of the leaf.

Photosynthesis

Plants need sunlight to grow and reproduce. Plants use the Sun's energy to make their own food. Remember, most of a plant's food is made in its leaves. Leaves are made of cells. Chloroplasts are inside these cells. Photosynthesis happens in the chloroplasts. **Photosynthesis** is the process that plants use to make sugar for food.

Plants need sunlight, water, and carbon dioxide for photosynthesis. Sunlight gives the cell the energy it needs for photosynthesis. A plant's roots get water from the soil. This water enters the chloroplasts. Carbon dioxide comes from the atmosphere. It enters the plant through its leaves. Carbon dioxide also enters the chloroplasts. The water and carbon dioxide are used to make sugar.

Photosynthesis makes oxygen. Some of this oxygen passes through the plant's leaves. It enters the atmosphere. Plants produce much of the oxygen in the atmosphere.

Photosynthesis also produces sugar. More sugar is made when sunlight reaches the chloroplast. This means that plants have more sugar during the day. They have less sugar at night. Plants use some of the sugar as food during the day. They also store some of the sugar. It is used at night. Plants turn some sugar into starch. Starch is a chemical. Do you eat food from plants? If so, you also eat the plant's sugars and starches. They give your cells energy.

Sugar is not only used for food. Sugars mix in plants to form cellulose. Cellulose is a chemical. It makes up a plant's strong cell walls.

Lesson 1 Checkpoint

1. What part of the leaf can best be compared to your skin?

_____

2. Describe the purpose and process of photosynthesis. How does the process change during a full day?

_____

_____

_____

_____

3. How does photosynthesis in plants benefit animals?

_____

_____

_____

4. **Cause and Effect** What is one cause of oxygen being found in the atmosphere?

_____

_____

_____

Lesson 2: How do stems and roots help a plant?

Vocabulary

xylem tubes that carry materials from the roots to the leaves

phloem tubes that carry sugar away from the leaves

Stems

Leaves grow on stems. Stems are plant organs. Stems hold leaves high. This way, the leaves can get more sunlight. Stems also hold fruit and flowers on plants. Some stems have thorns. A thorn is a sharp point. It protects the plant.

Xylem and Phloem

Some plants have tubes called xylem and phloem. These tubes are in the roots, stems, and leaves. Plants that have xylem and phloem are called vascular plants.

Xylem tissues are tubes. They carry water and minerals from the roots to the leaves. The roots take water from the soil. The water has minerals from the soil. Plant cells use minerals for photosynthesis.

Phloem tissues are tubes. They carry sugar from the leaves to the rest of the plant. The sugar is in water. In trees, phloem tissues are made below the tree's bark. New phloem tissues push old, dead phloem outward. Dead phloem make up a tree's bark. Bark protects the living phloem.

Kinds of Stems

There are two kinds of stems:
- Woody stems have lots of xylem tissue. Trees and shrubs have woody stems.
- Some stems are not woody. These stems are soft. They have less xylem. Pea plants and dandelions do not have woody stems.

Roots

Roots are plant organs. They grow in the ground. Roots are strong. They hold the plant in place. Roots also help the plant get water from the ground.

There are different kinds of root systems. Each kind of root has a different shape. Two kinds of roots are a taproot and a fibrous root.
- A taproot is large. It grows straight down. Small roots may grow out of the main taproot. Taproots may store food for the plant. Carrots, beets, and turnips are taproots.
- A fibrous root system has many roots. The roots grow out in all directions. They divide many times, and get smaller and smaller. A fibrous root system can look like an upside-down tree.

How do roots grow? There are special tissues near the root tips. New cells quickly form in these tissues. The new cells grow longer. They push the root tip farther into the ground.

Functions of Roots

Roots hold a plant in place. They may store food. Roots take in water and minerals from the soil. Plants use these materials to grow and reproduce. Plants also use water and minerals for repairs.

© Pearson Education, Inc. 5

Lesson 2 Checkpoint

1. What is the function of a plant's stem?

_____

_____

2. 🎯 **Cause and Effect** What causes bark to form on a tree?

_____

_____

_____

3. Explain how roots help a plant grow.

_____

_____

_____

4. What are the jobs of the phloem and xylem?

_____

_____

Name _____

Lesson 3: How do plants reproduce?

Vocabulary

pollen a grainy yellow powder containing sperm cells

pollination moving pollen from the stamen to the pistil

embryo a new plant inside a seed

spore a single plant cell that can develop into a new plant

Parts of the Flower

Some plants have flowers. Flowers are plant organs. A plant reproduces with flowers. Some plants can reproduce without flowers.

Some flowers have stamens and pistils. The stamen is the male part of a flower. A flower may have many stamens. **Pollen** is at the top of each stamen. Pollen is a yellow powder. It contains sperm cells. The pistil is the female part of a flower. A pistil is shaped like a bottle.

Passing Information

Plants need to reproduce before they die. Plants pass information to new plants. New plants will have the same shapes of flowers and leaves. This information is in DNA. DNA contains the information for making all parts of the plants.

Pollination

Pollination is moving pollen from the stamen to the pistil. Wind, water, insects, birds, and bats can move pollen.

After pollination, a tube grows from the pollen down to the pistil. Sperm cells move down the tube. They join with egg cells in the pistil. This is called fertilization.

DNA carries information about how a plant looks and works. The sperm cell has half of the male parent's DNA. The egg cell has half of the female parent's DNA. These cells make one whole set of DNA when they join. This causes new plants to look like their parents.

The fertilized egg grows and changes. It makes a seed with a tiny plant inside.

Going to Seed

A seed has three parts. It has a seed coat, an embryo, and endosperm. The seed coat protects the embryo. The **embryo** is the new plant inside a seed. Endosperm is the food stored in the embryo.

Spreading Seeds

Some plants have seeds that fall to the ground. These seeds grow near their parents.

Other seeds are spread to different places. Animals can spread these seeds. Animals eat fruit with seeds in it. The fruit passes through the digestive system of the animal. The seeds grow far from the parent plant.

The embryo will stay in the seed until the temperature and moisture outside are right. The life cycle of the seed begins. The seed grows into a mature plant. It can reproduce.

Reproducing Without Seeds

Many plants reproduce without sperm cells and egg cells. This is called asexual reproduction. There is only one parent in asexual reproduction. The offspring have the same DNA as the parent.

Some plants asexually reproduce by growing new plants from their stems or roots. Spider plants grow new plants on runners. Runners are long stems.

Another kind of asexual reproduction is budding. Small buds grow on a plant. The buds drop off and grow as new plants.

Mosses and ferns do not make flowers. These plants use spores to reproduce. A **spore** is a single plant cell that can grow into a new plant.

© Pearson Education, Inc. **5**

Lesson 3 Checkpoint

1. How are plant offspring like their parents? Why does this happen?

_____

_____

_____

2. Describe all the steps that occur during the making of a seed.

_____

_____

_____

_____

3. What is the life cycle of a plant that produces seeds?

_____

_____

_____

4. Compare and contrast sexual and asexual reproduction.

_____

_____

_____

5. Describe three methods of asexual reproduction.

_____

_____

_____

_____

_____

Lesson 4: How do plants grow?

Vocabulary

tropism a way that plants change their direction of growth in response to the environment

growth hormone a kind of chemical that affects plant growth

DNA and Growth

A seed sprouts when conditions are right. A seed will not grow if it is too cold or too dry. Different plants have different needs. A plant's DNA controls when and how it grows.

Plants grow in many shapes. Some trees are tall and thin. Some pine trees are shaped like cones. Some bushes are round. A plant's DNA controls the way its branches grow.

DNA affects how fast a plant grows. The environment also affects how a plant grows. A plant will grow more quickly if the environment has good conditions. The plant will grow more slowly if the environment has bad conditions. Bad conditions can include dry soil and cold air.

Tropisms

Plants can change the direction they grow in. They do this to meet their needs. For example, a plant's leaves may turn toward the Sun. A plant's roots may grow toward water. **Tropisms** are ways that plants change the direction they grow. Tropisms often happen when cells on one side of a plant grow faster than on the other side. This makes the stem bend. There are three kinds of tropisms:

- Gravitropism is a plant's growth toward or against gravity. Gravity is the pull of the Earth. Roots usually grow downward. They grow toward the pull of gravity. Stems usually grow upward. They grow against gravity.
- Phototropism is how a plant reacts to light. A stem might grow toward a light. Some plants turn their leaves toward light.
- Thigmotropism is a plant's growth due to touching an object. Thigmotropism can happen in stems or roots. Vine stems grow around posts or fences. This helps to support the plant. Roots may bend to grow away from rocks or hard soil.

Growth hormones can make cells grow faster or larger. A **growth hormone** is a chemical. Some cells have more growth hormone than others.

Water can also change the size of plant cells. Plant cells store water in vacuoles. Vacuoles can fill up with water and make the cell large. Vacuoles on one side of a plant might store more water than vacuoles on the other side of a plant. This can bend a plant.

Lesson 4 Checkpoint

1. Keisha plants a seed in moist, cold soil by her home. The seed does not sprout. What condition would you infer most likely needs to change for the seed to sprout?

_____

_____

_____

2. **Cause and Effect** What is the effect of different species of plants having very different DNA?

_____

_____

3. What is a growth hormone?

_____

_____

4. Explain how plants or plant parts grow toward light or grow upward.

_____

_____

_____

Lesson 1: What is an ecosystem?

Vocabulary

ecosystem all the living and nonliving things in an area

population a group of organisms of one species that live in an area at the same time

community the group of all the populations in an area

niche the role that an organism has in an ecosystem

habitat the place in which an organism lives

Living and Nonliving Parts

An **ecosystem** is all the living and nonliving things in an area. All of the living things in an ecosystem make up a **community.** A community has many different populations. A **population** is a group of organisms. All the organisms in a population are the same species. They live in the same area. One population in a forest might be the oak trees. Another population in a forest might be all of the red ants.

Ecosystems also have nonliving things. Air, water, soil, and sunlight are nonliving parts of an ecosystem. Organisms need these things to live. The kind and size of populations of organisms depends on the amount of air, water, soil, and sun in an ecosystem. The living and nonliving parts of an ecosystem work together. Each part of the system has a job.

Every population has needs. For example, organisms need food and space. When a population gets what it needs, it can live and grow. When a population does not get what it needs, it will get smaller. Some of the population might move away. Others might die.

Biomes

The world is divided into areas called biomes. A biome is a large ecosystem. The area of a biome has mostly the same climate and organisms. Biomes can be very large. One biome can cover many countries.

For example, one kind of biome is a rainforest. A rainforest biome is a place that has lots of rain and lots of plant growth. Some rainforests are very hot, such as the jungles of South America. But other rainforests can be quite cool, such as the temperate rainforests in Washington State.

The squirrels and trees are two parts of the temperate rainforest ecosystem. Trees help squirrels. They give squirrels food and shelter. But squirrels help trees, too. They spread seeds to help new trees grow. An ecosystem works because it has many parts and organisms that interact to meet their needs.

In an ecosystem, every organism has a niche and a habitat. A **niche** is the role of an organism in an ecosystem. For example, in a temperate rainforest, owls have a niche. They are hunters. They eat small animals like mice and chipmunks. A **habitat** is the place an organism lives. A habitat includes the soil, air, water, and plants. A spotted owl's habitat is the trees and the land where it lives.

All of the parts of an ecosystem work together and keep the ecosystem balanced. For example, the populations of owls and mice are balanced. If the number of mice goes down, owls will have less food. This will make the number of owls go down too. When there are fewer owls, the population of mice will begin to go up. In time, there will be more mice for owls to eat. Then the population of owls will go up too. The populations of owls and mice go up and down together. They balance.

Lesson 1 Checkpoint

1. Describe the parts of an ecosystem that organisms need.

   _____

   _____

   _____

2. 🎯 **Predict** What would happen to a community if half the water from an ecosystem was removed?

   _____

   _____

3. What is a population? What determines the kind and size of populations in an area?

   _____

   _____

   _____

4. Describe the parts of an ecosystem and tell how they maintain the system's balance.

   _____

   _____

   _____

Lesson 2: What are land biomes?

Tropical Rainforest Biomes

A tropical rainforest is a biome that is very warm and very wet. Ecosystems near the equator are warm all year long. Some of these places also get lots of rain. Many plants can grow in a tropical rainforest. They get plenty of water. A tropical rainforest has many kinds of plants and animals.

Organisms have parts that help them survive. For example, the kinkajou lives in rainforests. It has a long tail to grab branches. It has a long tongue to gather honey.

Deciduous Forest Biomes

A deciduous forest can grow in places with less rain. Deciduous forests have trees such as oaks, elms, and maples. These trees lose their leaves in the fall. Without leaves, these trees save food and water during the winter.

There are other changes during cold winter months. Many animals change their behavior in the winter. Bears in the deciduous forest sleep through the winter. Snakes, frogs, and salamanders stay underground. The fur of some brown rabbits changes to white fur. The white fur helps the rabbits blend in with the snow.

Grassland Biomes

Grasslands are biomes that are covered with many kinds of grasses. Grasslands do not have many trees. Two hundred years ago, large grasslands covered Midwest America. Today, most of these grasslands are farms.

Habitats often change. The climate can get hotter or colder. The amount of food or water can go up or down. When a habitat changes, animal populations often go down. For example, the gray wolf population has gone down. They live in grasslands. When grasslands were changed to farms, the wolves had less food and space. More people were hunting the wolves too. As a result, their population went down.

Taiga Biomes

Taigas are another kind of forest biome. Taigas are cold and dry. Taigas cover much of Canada and Russia. Most trees in taiga biomes have needles. These trees are evergreens. The needles are the parts of the tree that make food for the tree. Evergreens do not lose their needles in winter. This way, the tree is ready to make food as soon as it is warm enough for photosynthesis to happen. The needles have a waxy coating. This helps the tree to hold water during winter. Many animals in taiga communities use fur to keep warm.

Desert Biomes

A desert biome is very dry. Deserts get less than 25 centimeters of rain or snow each year. Organisms have special parts and behaviors to survive in the desert. Some desert plants have roots that are not very deep. They can take up any water from rain very quickly. Many desert animals nap during the hot hours of the day. They look for food during the cooler nights.

Tundra Biomes

The tundra is a very cold biome with little rain. There are many limiting factors in the tundra. A limiting factor is something that limits the number of organisms that can live in an ecosystem. Some limiting factors are the amount of food, water, or space. The long, cold winter is a limiting factor in the tundra. Plants can only grow during a very short warm season. Only small plants can grow. Small plants create less food to feed animals.

The carrying capacity is the number of organisms that can live in an ecosystem. If a population grows larger than the carrying capacity, organisms cannot meet their needs. This is called overcrowding.

Lesson 2 Checkpoint

1. Give examples of how an organism's behavior is related to changes in the deciduous forest biome.

_____

_____

_____

_____

2. What changes in a habitat would make a population get smaller?

_____

_____

_____

3. Explain how characteristics of an organism help it survive in a desert.

_____

_____

_____

4. What is the effect of a limiting factor on a population?

_____

_____

_____

Lesson 3: What are water ecosystems?

Rivers

Many animals live in river ecosystems. Some fish live in rivers. River ecosystems also include animals that spend most of their time on land. These animals have body parts that help them live on land or in the water. Otters have long, narrow bodies. Their bodies help them swim and catch fish. Otters can also close their nose and ears when under water.

Most plants and animals that live in rivers cannot live in oceans. Ocean water has much more salt than river water. Plants and animals in river ecosystems cannot live with the extra salt in ocean water.

Wetlands

A wetland is partly covered with water. Some wetlands are flooded for part of each year. There are many kinds of wetlands. Florida's Everglades is a large wetland. Alligators, fish, deer, snakes, and other animals live there. Swamps are wetlands with many trees and bushes.

Wetlands clean the water. Wetland plants, soil, and tiny organisms filter the water. This helps all organisms in the water.

Some wetlands are parts of estuaries. An estuary is a place where a river flows into an ocean. The water in estuaries is salty, but not as salty as the ocean.

Coral Reefs

Many ocean animals live near coral reefs. Corals are animals with a hard outside coating. They have a special relationship with algae. Algae are plant-like organisms. They grow inside the coral. Algae help the coral make their hard coating. As the corals grow and die, the hard coatings build up. They become a coral reef.

Algae need sunlight to grow. This means that algae will only grow in shallow, warm water. If the water is too deep, sunlight will not reach them. Coral needs water that is 18°C or warmer.

Coral reefs grow well in water that is low in nutrients and oxygen. Extra nutrients can help the coral's enemies grow. This can harm the coral reef.

The Deep Sea

The deeper parts of the ocean are cold and dark. Sunlight does not reach this deep water, so no plants can grow. Many animals there eat dead plants and animals that sink from above. In some places, bacteria make food from chemicals in the water. Bigger animals eat these bacteria.

The water pressure in deep water is very great. Animals bodies are adapted to live under this high pressure. Some clams, crabs, and tubeworms can live in deep sea ecosystems.

Lesson 3 Checkpoint

1. Where are estuaries found?

   _____

   _____

2. Why do coral live only in shallow water?

   _____

   _____

3. How does the type of water found in a water ecosystem affect the kind of organisms that live there?

   _____

   _____

   _____

Lesson 4: How do organisms interact?

Competition

Every organism needs things to stay alive. They need space, water, light, food, and mates. Organisms in an environment may compete for the things they need. They might fight to get the same food, water, or space.

Animals sometimes compete with others in the same species. Two fish might compete for food in the same river.

Animals in different species also compete. Rabbits and mice in a dry desert compete when they search for plants to eat. Cats and dogs might compete for territory. Territory is land.

Plants also compete. They compete for sunlight and water. The kudzu vine was brought to the South in 1876. This plant grows very quickly. It covers other plants so they cannot get enough sunlight. The covered plants cannot move, so they die.

Plants compete for water too. Plants with bigger roots can get more water.

Symbiosis

Different kinds of animals can have many different relationships. Symbiosis is a relationship between two different species. There are four kinds of symbiosis.

In the first kind of symbiosis, one animal is helped. The other animal is not affected. The buffalo and the cattle egret have this kind of relationship. The cattle egret is a bird. It often eats near a buffalo. When the buffalo eats grass, it scares insects in the grass. The bird stays near the buffalo and eats the insects that hop away. In this relationship, the bird is helped. The buffalo is not helped or hurt.

In the second kind of symbiosis, both animals are helped. For example, some microorganisms live inside the buffalo. They live in its digestive system. The organisms help the buffalo break down the food it eats. The organisms are helped too. They get food to eat.

In a third kind of symbiosis, one animal is helped and the other is hurt. A parasite is an organism. It feeds off another organism. The organism the parasite feeds off of is called the host. For example, worms sometimes live in the buffalo's blood. These parasites eat food inside the buffalo's body. They can also use oxygen. Parasites can make the buffalo weak or sick. Sometimes, they even kill the buffalo.

In the fourth kind of symbiosis, one organism cannot live without a partner. The organisms need each other to stay alive. A lichen is one example. A lichen is a fungus with a bacteria or algae growing inside. The bacteria or algae make food from sunlight. The fungus uses this food. The bacteria or algae get a safe home inside the fungus.

Lesson 4 Checkpoint

1. Describe why organisms compete and what the results of competition might be.

_____

_____

_____

2. Describe the symbiosis between a parasite and its host.

_____

_____

_____

3. Give an example of a relationship where both organisms are helped.

_____

_____

_____

4. ◎ **Predict** Suppose a veterinarian gave a buffalo some medicine that killed all organisms inside the buffalo. Predict what effects this would have on the buffalo.

_____

_____

_____

Lesson 5: How does energy move in ecosystems?

Vocabulary

energy pyramid a diagram that shows the amounts of energy that flow through each level of a food chain

Food Chains and Webs

Every organism needs food to live. Food gives energy to organisms. Energy in an ecosystem moves from one organism to another. Food chains and food webs show how energy moves in an ecosystem.

Producers are organisms that make their own food. Plants and some very small organisms are producers. All producers make their own food for energy. They use energy from sunlight or chemicals in nature to make their own food. The niche of producers is to use energy from the Sun to make food. Some animals eat plants to get energy.

Consumers cannot make their own food. They usually eat other organisms to stay alive and grow. All animals are consumers.

Some animals eat plants. They are called herbivores. Some animals eat other animals. They are called carnivores. Omnivores eat both plants and animals. Decomposers eat waste or dead organisms.

When an animal eats food, it gets energy from the food. The energy moves from the food to the animal. The arrows in a food chain show how energy moves. For example, one food chain shows that energy comes from the Sun. Plants use this energy to make food. Rabbits eat plants. Owls eat the rabbits. Bacteria eat the owls when they die.

On land, almost all food chains begin with plants. In the ocean, almost all food chains begin with plankton. Plankton are very small organisms that are like plants.

There are many relationships in an ecosystem. A food chain shows only one chain. A food web can show more relationships. A food web combines many food chains.

Energy Pyramids

An **energy pyramid** shows how much energy there is at each level of a food chain. Look at the energy pyramid on pages 146–147 of your textbook. Producers are at the bottom. They have the most energy. As you go up from producers to herbivores and carnivores, the pyramid gets smaller. This shows that less energy flows through those levels.

Why doesn't energy reach the next level? Some of the energy is used. For example, a rabbit gets energy by eating plants. When an owl eats the rabbit, only part of the plant's energy is still in the rabbit. The rest of the plant's energy did not disappear. It was turned into other kinds of energy. The rabbit used this energy to run, breathe, and think. These activities turned the food into the energy of body heat. This heat energy did not move to the next level of the energy pyramid.

© Pearson Education, Inc. 5

Lesson 5 Checkpoint

1. What is the niche, or role, of a producer?

_____

_____

2. Explain how an energy pyramid shows the flow of energy in a food chain or food web.

_____

_____

_____

_____

3. Explain why animals' food and energy can be traced back to plants and the Sun.

_____

_____

_____

4. Why do animals eat?

_____

_____

Lesson 6: What cycles occur in ecosystems?

Vocabulary

cycle a repeating process or a repeating flow of material through a
system

Recycling Matter

Waste builds up in every ecosystem. Animals make waste every day. Plants and animals also become waste when they die.

Most decomposers are very small organisms, like bacteria and fungi. Worms, flies, slime molds, and slugs are also decomposers. Decomposers eat waste and dead material. Decomposers recycle some of this waste. This is an important role. It is their niche in the ecosystem.

Decomposers eat waste. They break it into smaller pieces. Then they put it back into the soil. They put minerals from waste back in the earth. Then other organisms can use these minerals.

Fire also breaks down some dead material. When plants burn, the ashes go into the soil.

Nitrogen Cycle

Plant and animal cells all need a gas called nitrogen. Nitrogen cycles through food chains. Most organisms cannot use nitrogen from the air. They can only use nitrogen compounds. Nitrogen compounds are chemicals that contain nitrogen.

Lightning can produce nitrogen compounds. The high temperature of lightning can cause nitrogen to combine with other gases. These nitrogen compounds fall to Earth when it rains.

Some bacteria make nitrogen compounds. They make nitrogen compounds and put them in the soil. Plants collect the compounds with their roots. Some rainforest plants can also make nitrogen compounds. Their roots can take nitrogen from the air.

Herbivores get nitrogen when they eat plants. Carnivores get nitrogen when they eat herbivores. Nitrogen returns to the soil or air when animals die. It also returns to soil in animals' waste. Decomposers change animals' nitrogen into nitrogen that plants can use. Farmers also add nitrogen to the soil to help plants grow.

Carbon Dioxide and Oxygen

Every ecosystem has a cycle of carbon dioxide and oxygen. Plants take in carbon dioxide and give off oxygen. Animals take in oxygen and give off carbon dioxide. Some oxygen combines with materials like iron. This removes the oxygen from the air. But the cycle is not that simple. The diagram on pages 152–153 in your textbook shows more steps in this cycle.

Plants make oxygen by photosynthesis. Some other organisms also produce oxygen. In the ocean, there are very small organisms called plankton. Plankton use photosynthesis to produce oxygen.

There are two major ways carbon dioxide enters an ecosystem. They are respiration and combustion.

In respiration, cells combine oxygen with food. Respiration produces carbon dioxide and water. Plants and animals live by respiration.

Combustion happens when something burns. Combustion takes oxygen from the air and produces carbon dioxide. Some combustion is natural, like forest fires. Other combustion takes place in machines like cars and home heaters.

Lesson 6 Checkpoint

1. What is the niche of slime molds and other decomposers?

_____

_____

2. Describe how matter cycles through an ecosystem.

_____

_____

_____

3. Describe three ways that oxygen gas is removed from the atmosphere and used.

_____

_____

_____

4. How is lightning helpful to organisms?

_____

_____

Lesson 1: How do ecosystems change?

Animals Change Ecosystems

Ecosystems are always changing. Some changes are quick. Some are very slow. Animals cause some of these changes. For example, locusts are insects. They travel in large groups called swarms. A swarm of locusts can eat many plants. Then there is less food for people and animals.

Beavers change a stream ecosystem by building a dam. Dams stop water from flowing. This makes a pond ecosystem. The beavers are safe from other animals in the pond. A few other animals can also live in the pond. But a few animals are hurt by the pond. It floods their homes.

Sometimes, changes in ecosystems can be helpful. Worms slowly dig holes in the soil. This brings oxygen to plant roots.

People Change Ecosystems

People change ecosystems in many ways. They build houses and cut down forests. They throw garbage into ecosystems. They bring new plants and animals into an ecosystem. A new species causes changes to an ecosystem. These changes can effect an entire species.

For example, ships carried the zebra mussel to the United States. Zebra mussels did not have predators in their new habitat. So the population of zebra mussels grew very quickly. The large numbers of zebra mussels use space and food needed by other species.

Plants can change ecosystems too. Early settlers brought the garlic mustard plant to the United States. Animals do not eat this plant. The plant grows quickly. It can keep other plants from getting enough water and sunlight.

People's actions change ecosystems too. Americans make more than 200 million tons of garbage every year. Most garbage is put in a landfill. A landfill is a pile of garbage covered with soil and grass. An ecosystem changes a lot when a landfill is being used. The ecosystem changes again after the landfill is covered. It might return to the way it was before the landfill. In the past, landfills leaked pollution into nearby lakes and ponds. Today, liners keep the garbage from leaking into the ground.

People create air pollution. Some air pollution makes acid rain. Acid rain pollutes soils and lakes. Acid rain can kill plants and animals. People can treat polluted lakes by adding helpful chemicals to the water.

Lesson 1 Checkpoint

1. Explain how changes in an ecosystem can sometimes be helpful and
sometimes harmful.

_____

_____

_____

2. Why can populations of zebra mussels and garlic mustard grow so
quickly in their new ecosystems?

_____

_____

3. How do beaver ponds help the beaver? How do they affect other
organisms?

_____

_____

Lesson 2: How do species change?

Vocabulary

inherit when offspring get their parents' genes

mutation a change in an organism's genes

structural adaptation body part that helps the organism survive

behavioral adaptation inherited behavior that helps an animal survive

Inheriting DNA

Some ecosystem changes happen over many years. Some of these changes happen because offspring are not exactly like their parents. Plants and animals **inherit** half of their genes from each parent. Genes are also called DNA. They decide almost everything about how an organism grows.

Every animal gets a mix of genes from both parents. That is why every animal is different. Some offspring will be taller than their parents. Some will be shorter. Some will have different color eyes. But most things will be the same. Think about a puppy. The puppy has the same organs as its parents. It has the same number of legs. It has the same kind of fur. The color of its fur might be different.

Traits Not Inherited

Genes affect an animal's growth. But the environment also plays a role. Ecosystems affect how plants and animals grow. A plant may not grow well if there is very little food and water. An animal might not grow well if the weather is very hot or very cold.

Ecosystems can also change an organism's color. The American flamingo is born with white feathers. Its feathers turn pink or red when it eats small crustaceans like shrimp.

Adaptations

Sometimes a change happens in an organism's genes. This change is called a **mutation.** Mutations can be helpful, harmful, or neither. Mutations are often harmful. For example, an animal might be born without the ability to make white blood cells. Other mutations are helpful. A helpful mutation makes an organism adapt to fit into an ecosystem more successfully.

Structural Adaptations

Structural adaptations are changed body parts that help an organism live in its environment. For example, a hummingbird with a longer beak might be able to get food from deep flowers. The long beak is a structural adaptation. This bird might survive even when there is little rain. It can get more food than the other hummingbirds. The bird might pass this mutation to its offspring. In time, a large part of the hummingbird population may have this kind of long beak. The process of a species developing adaptations is called natural selection. It helps organisms survive in different ecosystems.

Behavioral Adaptations

Behavioral adaptations are behaviors that help animals survive. Sometimes they are called instinct. Behavioral adaptations affect how an animal behaves around other animals. For example, bees and ants use instinct to work together. Desert animals are active at night when it is cooler. This is another example of a behavioral adaptation.

Animals do not inherit all their behaviors. They learn some behaviors. For example, lions do not know how to hunt when they are born. Lion parents teach their offspring how to hunt. Monkeys teach their offspring different ways to get food.

© Pearson Education, Inc. 5

Lesson 2 Checkpoint

1. What are some characteristics that are determined by DNA? What are some characteristics that are influenced by the ecosystem?

_____

_____

2. How are behavioral adaptations like structural adaptations? How are they different?

_____

_____

3. What are two reasons that an animal will not have the same DNA as its mother?

_____

_____

Lesson 3: How do changes cause more changes?

Vocabulary

pesticide a poison that kills insects

extinct when there are no members of a kind of organism left alive

Changes in Behavior

Changes in one part of an ecosystem effect other parts. Animals may change their behavior when other animals in their ecosystem change. For example, a cat might change its habits when a new puppy arrives. The cat might spend more time sitting on chairs or tables to keep away from the puppy.

Changes in Populations

Some populations can adapt to changes in their ecosystems. Think about mosquitoes. People use chemicals called **pesticides** to kill mosquitoes. However, a few mosquitoes might have unusual genes that make them able to live with the pesticide. Their offspring often have these genes too. They will survive and reproduce.

Bacteria can also adapt to changes in their environment. Some bacteria cause diseases. Antibiotics are medicines that can kill these bacteria. However, some bacteria are able to survive. They adapt to living around antibiotics. This makes the antibiotics less effective.

Extinction

What happens when a plant or animal cannot adapt to harmful changes? The plant or animal must move to another place. However, moving is not always possible. For example, plants cannot move to another place. This causes their population to get smaller. Some species may even become extinct. A species that is **extinct** has no members of its kind alive.

Fossils show that many plants and animals no longer exist. Species have become extinct through natural processes and human acts

The dodo is an extinct bird. The dodo could not fly. It lived on an island. Sailors brought pigs and monkeys to the island. The dodo could not fly away to safety. These new predators killed the birds. The dodo became extinct around 1680.

In the United States, the bald eagle almost became extinct. DDT is a pesticide. It was used to kill insects on farms. DDT went into lakes and streams when it rained. Soon, fish had DDT in their bodies. Bald eagles ate the fish. The DDT made eagle eggs very thin. The shells often broke before the young bird was ready to hatch. Other eggs did not hatch at all. This made the eagle population go down. It seemed that eagles would disappear from most of the country.

People were not allowed to use DDT anymore. The bald eagle population started to grow again.

© Pearson Education, Inc. 5

Lesson 3 Checkpoint

1. Explain how a species of mosquitoes can become adapted to having pesticides in their ecosystem.

   _____

   _____

   _____

2. What do fossils teach us about extinction?

   _____

   _____

3. Which is more likely to develop adaptations to a changing ecosystem: a population that often has many mutations or a population that has few mutations?

   _____

   _____

4. ⦿ **Cause and Effect** What was the cause of the bald eagle population getting smaller?

   _____

   _____

Lesson 1: How can the oceans be described?

Vocabulary

salinity a measure of how salty water is

The Hydrosphere

All the waters of Earth make up the hydrosphere. Almost all of the hydrosphere is ocean water. Only 3/100 of the hydrosphere is in other places.

Oceans cover almost 3/4 of Earth and all the oceans are connected. The Pacific Ocean is the deepest ocean. Its average depth is about 4,000 meters. Its deepest place is more than 11,000 meters deep.

The Pacific Ocean is also the largest ocean. It is followed by the Atlantic Ocean, the Indian Ocean, and the Arctic Ocean. Look at the map on pages 200–201 in your textbook. It shows how the oceans are connected, their shapes, and their sizes.

The oceans are all different from each other. Some have more storms than others. The water can also be different. Some water may have more salt than others. Some water may be warmer than others.

Salinity

Rivers dissolve salts from rocks and soil and carry the salts to the ocean.

Salinity is a measure of how salty water is. Ocean water is saltier in some places than in others. Places where rivers pour fresh water into the ocean have low salinity. Salinity is higher in warmer places. Why? Ocean water evaporates quickly in warm temperatures leaving the salt behind.

Cold water with high salinity is heavier than either warm water or water with a lower salinity. Some ocean currents are caused by cold salty water sinking under warmer water. Other currents are caused by winds. The map on pages 200–201 in your textbook shows currents on the surface of the ocean water. Currents below the surface of the water flow in different ways.

Temperature

The temperature of ocean water varies from place to place. Ocean water near the equator is warm while ocean water near the poles is colder.

The water is not always colder just because it is farther north. Some currents carry warm water toward the poles. For example, the Gulf Stream moves warm water from the Caribbean Sea to the North Atlantic Ocean. Other currents carry cold water toward the equator. For example, the California Current carries cold water south along the coast of the United States.

Ocean Resources

The ocean is the source of many products we use. We get fish from the ocean. We also get much of our salt from the ocean. Drinking water also comes from the ocean. But people can drink ocean water only if the salt is taken out of it. Taking salt out of ocean water is expensive. This is why it is not very common.

© Pearson Education, Inc. 5

Lesson 1 Checkpoint

1. How much of Earth is covered by water?

_____

_____

2. Use the map on pages 200–201 of your textbook to describe the shape, size, and connections of Earth's oceans.

_____

_____

3. What is salinity? What causes some ocean water to have a higher salinity than other ocean water?

_____

_____

_____

Lesson 2: Where is fresh water found?

Vocabulary

aquifer the layer of rock and soil that groundwater flows through

water table the top level of groundwater in an aquifer

reservoir a lake that forms behind a dam

Fresh Water

Drinking water is called fresh water. Fresh water has some salt, but it has much less salt than ocean water.

Almost all fresh water starts as rain or snow. Some of this fresh water sinks into the ground. Some goes into rivers and lakes. Some fresh water is frozen in ice and glaciers. The amount of fresh water is limited. Water should be used wisely.

Groundwater

Groundwater is rain or melted snow that soaks into the ground. An **aquifer** is the layer of rock and soil that groundwater flows through. The top level of groundwater in an aquifer is the **water table.** The water table rises when it rains or snows. It becomes lower when there is not much water in the area. It also becomes lower when people use too much water.

Rivers

Rivers, lakes, and streams are surface waters. Melting snow, rainwater, and groundwater all help form Earth's surface waters. Water from rain and melting snow flows in small streams. These small streams join together to form larger streams and rivers. The area from which water drains into a river is called the river's watershed.

What happens to a watershed can affect places far away. Chemicals that are placed in the watershed can be carried by water to rivers. These chemicals can cause changes to ecosystems downstream.

Lakes

Lakes form when water collects in a low area. Dams can also cause lakes to form. A dam stops water from flowing. This causes the water to collect in the low spot. A **reservoir** is a lake that forms behind a dam.

Ice

About 7/10 of Earth's fresh water is frozen in ice. Much of Earth's ice is on Greenland and Antarctica. Huge ice sheets cover most of these lands. Smaller areas of ice are called glaciers.

Ice sheets and glaciers form when each year's snowfall is greater than the amount of snow that melts. The weight of the new snow squeezes the snow into ice.

Some glaciers and ice sheets reach the ocean. Large pieces of ice can break off in these places. These floating pieces of ice are called icebergs.

Getting Water to Homes

Fresh water can contain harmful bacteria or chemicals. The water must be treated before we use it. It must be pumped to a treatment plant where chemicals are added to the water. Dirt sticks to particles in the chemicals. The particles get heavy. They sink to the bottom of a tank. Next, the water passes through filters. Filters remove small particles that did not settle earlier. More chemicals are added to the water. This treated water is pumped to the top of a water tower. Gravity pulls water down from the tank. The water flows through pipes to our homes.

Lesson 2 Checkpoint

1. How is fresh water different from ocean water?

_____

_____

2. How much of Earth's fresh water is in icebergs and glaciers?

_____

3. How do icebergs form?

_____

_____

4. **Sequence** the steps in treating water before it gets to a town's water tower.

_____

_____

_____

Lesson 3: What is the water cycle?

Vocabulary

evaporation the changing of liquid water to water vapor

condensation water vapor turning into liquid

precipitation water that falls from clouds as rain, snow, sleet or hail

sublimation ice changing into water vapor without first melting

Water in the Air

There is always water in the air. This water is a gas called water vapor. There are many kinds of gas particles in the air. They move in all directions. Air pressure is the pressure of these gas particles against another object.

The Water Cycle

Water is always moving. It moves on Earth's surface. It moves underground. It also moves in the air as water vapor. Water moves through the environment in different forms. It can change from one form to another in the water cycle.

Temperature, pressure, and the height of the land can affect the steps of the water cycle. The four steps of the water cycle are: evaporation, condensation, precipitation, and runoff. **Evaporation** is the changing of liquid water to water vapor. In **condensation** the water vapor turns back into a liquid such as water droplets in clouds. This liquid can form clouds. Condensation also forms dew. In **precipitation**, the water falls from clouds as rain, snow, sleet, or hail. This water flows downhill into rivers, lakes, or oceans. This movement is called runoff.

The picture on pages 208–209 of your textbook show the steps in the water cycle. But this picture does not show every step. For example, sublimation is another path in the water cycle. **Sublimation** is ice changing into water vapor without first melting. Sublimation takes place much more slowly than evaporation.

Many Paths of the Water Cycle

Not all water stays in the water cycle. Water is made and used by living things. Organisms produce water when they breathe. Plants use water during photosynthesis. Water vapor rises up and can form a cloud.

Energy in the Water Cycle

Energy from the Sun keeps the water cycle going. It causes most melting, evaporation, and sublimation. Sunlight also helps water vapor rise. Water releases heat when it condenses. This heat warms the air or water in the surrounding area.

Lesson 3 Checkpoint

1. How are evaporation and condensation the same? How are they different?

_____

_____

_____

_____

2. What factors affect evaporation and condensation?

_____

_____

3. 🎯 **Sequence** two ways that water moves from precipitation through part of the water cycle and returns to precipitation.

_____

_____

_____

_____

_____

Lesson 4: How do clouds form?

Vocabulary

sleet frozen rain drops

Temperature and Pressure

Clouds may form in many shapes and sizes. Clouds form when water vapor changes into small ice crystals or tiny drops of water.

Temperature affects clouds. If the air temperature near the cloud is high, the cloud will be made of water drops. If the air temperature is low, it will be made of ice crystals.

Air pressure also affects clouds. Many clouds form when air moves up to areas with less air pressure. Since there is less pressure, air expands and cools. If the air cools enough, water vapor forms ice crystals or droplets.

Types of Clouds

- Cirrus clouds are high-altitude clouds that form above 6,000 meters. They are thin and white.

- Vertical clouds grow up and down. They have air rising in them. They are sometimes called thunderheads because often cause thunderstorms.

- Altocumulus clouds are mid-altitude clouds that begin between 2,000 and 7,000 meters above the ground. They look like small puffy balls. The bottoms of these clouds can look dark because sunlight may not reach them. The sides are white because they reflect sunlight.

- Stratus clouds are low-altitude clouds that form less than 2,000 meters above the ground. They cover the whole sky. They look dark because most sunlight cannot get through the layer of clouds.

- Fog is a cloud at ground level. It can form on clear, cool nights with no wind. If the air near the ground is cool enough, water vapor collects into tiny droplets. This creates a cloud near the ground that can get larger if more droplets form.

Precipitation

Most rain in the United States starts as snow. The air temperature high above the ground is often below 0°C. Clouds of ice crystals form in the cold air. The air temperature between the cloud and the ground affects the precipitation.

If this temperature is below 0°C, the ice crystals will not melt. They will fall to the ground as snow. If the air is warmer than 0°C, the ice crystals will melt. They will fall to the ground as rain.

The ice crystals melt as they fall through a layer of warm air. But if the air near the ground is very cold, rain can freeze before it hits the ground. The frozen raindrops are **sleet.**

Hail Formation

Hail forms when strong winds blow raindrops up into a cloud. The air at the top of the cloud is freezing cold, creating a small piece of ice. The wind blows the ice through the cloud many times. Layers of water freeze on it. When it gets too heavy for the winds to carry, it falls to the ground. Most hail is about the size of a pea. Some hail is bigger than a baseball.

Lesson 4 Checkpoint

1. What are clouds and fog made of?

_____

_____

2. How does sleet form?

_____

_____

3. What happens to snow if it falls through a layer of warm air?

_____

_____

4. **Sequence** the steps taken from water vapor to sleet.

_____

_____

_____

_____

Lesson 1: How does air move?

Vocabulary

convection current when gases or liquids rise and sink in a circular path

Layers of Air

Do you know what is in the air you breathe? Air is made of gases. About 8/10 of air is nitrogen. About 2/10 of air is oxygen. The rest of the air is carbon dioxide, water, and other gases. Earth is the only planet with this kind of air.

The atmosphere of Earth has five layers. The temperature changes as you go up through the layers. As you go higher, the altitude increases and the air pressure gets lower. Altitude is how high you are in the atmosphere. Air pressure is the amount of air. The higher you are in the atmosphere, the lower the air pressure is. The air pressure changes because the gas particles in the air are farther apart. The higher you go, the less air there is above you.

Convection Currents

Have you ever put your feet in a lake to cool them off? Sunlight warms up land quickly, but it takes longer to warm up water. At night, land cools off faster than water. This is why the air above land and the air above water are different temperatures.

Convection currents form when there are different air temperatures. A convection current happens when gases or liquids rise and sink in a circular path.

Gas particles are closer together in cool air. Gas particles are farther apart in warm air.

This makes cool air heavier than warm air. When warm and cool air are next to each other, the cool air sinks and the warm air rises. This is what happens to convection currents near the ocean at night.

There are six very large convection currents in the air over Earth. The convection currents over North America and the spinning of Earth cause wind patterns. In North America, this makes the wind blow mainly from west to east.

There are jet streams high above the ground. A jet stream is a very high fast wind. The different temperatures between the convection currents form jet streams. Jet streams can change the temperature, winds, and rain because it affects air movement.

Lesson 1 Checkpoint

1. As altitude increases, how does air pressure change? Why?

_____

_____

_____

_____

2. What causes convection currents?

_____

_____

3. In what direction do winds of North America generally blow?

_____

_____

4. 🎯 **Draw Conclusions** At night, land cools more than water. Air above land will be cooler than air above the water. What conclusion can you draw about convection currents near the ocean at night?

_____

_____

Lesson 2: What are air masses?

Vocabulary

air mass a large body of air with similar properties all through it

front a boundary between two air masses

Kinds of Air Masses

When air stays in one area for a long time, it takes on properties of that area. It becomes an **air mass.** An air mass is a large body of air with similar properties through it. The air mass keeps these properties even after it moves away from the area.

Weather is often caused by air masses. If it is warm and sunny, it will stay that way until a new air mass moves to the area. Some types of weather only happen at the edges of air masses.

There are different types of air masses. Maritime polar air masses form over the oceans near the poles. These air masses are cold and moist. Maritime tropical air masses form over warm oceans or rainforests. These air masses are warm and wet. Continental polar air masses form over land near the poles. These air masses are cold and dry. Continental tropical air masses form over hot deserts. These air masses are warm and dry.

Air masses move because of winds. The winds may be close to the ground or high like the jet stream. If a jet stream brings air from Canada to the United States, the weather will probably get colder.

When Air Masses Meet

A **front** is a boundary between two air masses. Air masses usually move from west to east over North America. Fronts have the same movement.

Fronts are named for the kind of air they bring to an area. A cold front brings colder air. A warm front brings warmer air. A stationary front does not move very much. It stays in the same area for a while.

Fronts often have rising warm air. This makes the areas near the fronts have low air pressure. Areas in the middle of the air mass have higher air pressure. The rising air at fronts causes precipitation such as rain or snow.

Lesson 2 Checkpoint

1. How do air masses form and move?

_____

_____

2. Why does precipitation often happen at fronts?

_____

_____

3. Suppose one morning, you need a light coat to play outside.
A thunderstorm forces you to go inside for several hours. That
afternoon, you need a heavy coat to go outside. What kind of front
has passed?

_____

_____

4. 🎯 **Draw Conclusions** An air mass moves into the middle of
North America. It has low humidity and high temperatures. Where
can you conclude that this air mass formed?

_____

_____

Lesson 3: What causes severe weather?

Thunderstorms

There are different kinds of severe weather. Thunderstorms, hurricane, tornados, and blizzards are all examples of severe weather. Severe weather can be dangerous. It is important to get ready for severe weather if you know it is coming.

Thunderstorms form in stages. The first stage of a thunderstorm has strong, quickly rising currents of moist air. This air forms big clouds. The clouds have both water droplets and ice crystals.

During stage two of a thunderstorm rain falls. Some air is pulled down with the rain. This causes the storm to have currents moving up and down.

During the third and final stage of a thunderstorm, all the currents move down. The clouds get smaller as the rain falls from them.

Tornados

The weather has to happen in a certain way for a tornado to form. First, layers of wind blow at different speeds in different directions. Between these layers, a column of air starts to spin on its side. One end of this column is lifted by upward winds. The other end is pushed down by downward winds. The spinning column of air is a funnel cloud. When it reaches the ground, it is called a tornado.

Tornados often last only a few minutes. However, their path can be very long and wide. Winds in a tornado move so fast they can even throw a car around!

Tornados are very dangerous. If you know a tornado is coming, take shelter. A basement is the best place to go. A closet or a windowless room are good places too.

Hurricanes

Warm ocean water has a lot of energy in it. When water vapor from the warm oceans condenses, energy is released. Sometimes this energy grows and powers the winds of a hurricane.

A hurricane's winds are slower than a tornado's winds, but a hurricane usually does more damage. This is because hurricanes last for days. They are also much wider than tornados and can hit several countries. Hurricanes also cause huge waves. The ocean can rise and flood the shores. Heavy rains can also cause floods inland.

If you know a hurricane is coming, here are some ways to get ready. Put boards over your windows. Test your flashlights and battery-powered radios. Store valuable things in plastic containers high off the ground. When the hurricane gets close, it is important to stay inside or leave immediately if the authorities ask people to evacuate.

Lesson 3 Checkpoint

1. List four examples of severe weather.

_____

_____

_____

2. **Sequence** What happens in each the of three stages that a thunderstorm might have?

_____

_____

_____

3. What is the cause of a tornado?

_____

_____

4. What are the effects of a hurricane?

_____

_____

_____

Lesson 4: How are weather forecasts made?

Vocabulary

anemometer a tool used to measure wind speed

barometer a tool used to measure air pressure

rain gauge a tool used to measure how much rain has fallen

Collecting Data

A weather system has many parts. A weather system has temperature, moisture, clouds, precipitation, wind speed, and wind direction. In a weather system, these parts may work with each other and often change. We use tools to learn about these parts.

A **barometer** shows air pressure. An **anemometer** measures wind speed. A hygrometer measures the moisture in the air. A **rain gauge** measures how much rain has fallen. People use radar to measure the winds and rain inside a storm. People use the data from all these tools to describe a weather system.

Weather Forecasts

Weather forecasters look at how the temperature changes with the seasons. They look at patterns of snowfall and rainfall. Forecasters study weather patterns to learn more about how land, air, and the water cycle affect the weather.

Weather forecasters look at many patterns of weather change. There are patterns in the seasons of the year. There are even patterns during each day.

Weather forecasters expect the current weather to act the same way that weather has acted in the past. The more information forecasters have, the more accurate the forecast will be.

Forecasters show current weather and predictions on weather maps. Their maps show which way a front is moving. In the United States, fronts move from west to east. Fronts are always in areas of low pressure. Areas around fronts are often cloudy. Areas of high pressure that are away from fronts often have clear skies.

Lesson 4 Checkpoint

1. What are the parts of a weather system?

   _____

   _____

2. Read the weather map on page 245 of your textbook. What was the weather like in your part of the country when this map was made?

   _____

   _____

3. What kind of weather system is found in areas of high pressure? Low air pressure?

   _____

   _____

Lesson 5: What is climate?

Vocabulary

climate the average of weather conditions over a long time, usually thirty years

Weather and Climate

Do you know the difference between weather and climate? Weather is all the conditions in one place at one time. Weather can change from day to day. **Climate** is the average of weather conditions over a long time. Climate includes the average amount of rain, the average temperature, and how much temperature changes in a year.

Landforms Affect Climate

Mountains may have different climates than the low areas near them. Higher land is cooler than the lower land around mountains. The opposite sides of a mountain can also have different climates. In the United States, the west side of the Cascade Mountains is wet. But the east side of the mountains has a dry climate. This is because the air does not have as much moisture in it when it reaches the east side.

Do you remember that water warms and cools more slowly than land? This causes the temperature near water to change more slowly than the temperature inland.

Oceans Affect Climate

Ocean currents can also make a climate warmer or cooler. Big currents carry warm water north. Some of the warm water evaporates and makes the wind above it warmer. Those winds blow over land, making its climate warmer. Big ocean currents also carry cold water south. The cold water cools the winds. These winds make the climate cooler.

Past Climates

Climates are the average weather conditions over a long time. But climates do change. In the 1600s the climate of North America and Europe were much colder and wetter than they are now. This time is called the Little Ice Age.

Climates have changed many times. Sometimes they change quickly and sometimes they change slowly. Scientists study fossils to learn about climates from long ago. If a plant fossil looks like a modern plant, scientists guess the two plants need the same climate. If the modern plant needs water and the plant fossil was found in a desert, scientists guess the climate might have changed.

How Climates Change

Many things can cause a climate to change. The Little Ice Age may have been caused by the Sun making less energy. An erupting volcano or an asteroid hitting the Earth can cause a sudden climate change. This is because the volcano and the asteroid release materials into the atmosphere that block or reflect sunlight. The climate becomes cooler.

Warmer climates may be caused by carbon dioxide, methane, and water vapor in the atmosphere. Burning coal and using gasoline releases these things into the air.

Scientists talk about the changes in climates. They do not always agree on why a climate changed. Scientists work very hard to understand why a climate changed.

© Pearson Education, Inc. 5

Lesson 5 Checkpoint

1. How does weather differ from climate?

_____

_____

2. How are fossils used to study past climates?

_____

_____

_____

3. What can cause a sudden climate change?

_____

_____

_____

Lesson 1: What is the structure of Earth?

Vocabulary

crust Earth's outermost and thinnest layer

mantle below the crust, this layer makes up most of Earth's material

core the center of Earth

Earth has four layers. They are called the crust, the mantle, the outer core, and the inner core. Each layer has its own properties.

The Crust

The **crust** is the outside layer. The crust is also the thinnest layer. There are two kinds of crust: continental crust and oceanic crust. Continental crust makes up the lands of the continents.

Oceanic crust lies below most of the ocean floor. Continental crust and oceanic crust meet underwater. The continental crust dips underwater to form the continental shelf. Then the edge of the continental shelf drops down to form the continental slope. The continental rise is at the bottom of this slope. This is the beginning of oceanic crust.

The Mantle and Core

The **mantle** is below the crust. The mantle is the thickest layer of Earth. The top of the mantle is made of partially melted rock. The crust and the top of the mantle make up the lithosphere. The lithosphere covers Earth like a thin shell. Most of the lithosphere is under the oceans of the hydrosphere.

The deeper part of the mantle is under very high pressure. Its temperature ranges from 900°C to 2,200°C. The mantle is made of solid rock. Earth's forces push on this rock. This makes the rock bend and flow like a thick liquid. Slow convection currents move the rock in the mantle. Cooler rock flows down. Hotter rock flows up. High temperatures inside Earth provide the energy for these currents to move. The lithosphere floats on top of these convection currents in the mantle.

The **core** is at the center of Earth. It is made mostly of iron. The temperature can be 5,000°C. The inner core is solid. The outer core is liquid. This liquid moves in currents. These currents make Earth's magnetic field.

Scientists cannot go to the mantle or the core to study them. These layers are too deep. But, scientists have other ways to learn about these layers. One way is by studying mantle material that has pushed up through cracks in the crust. This happens in some places in the ocean floor.

Scientists also use earthquakes to study Earth's layers. Earthquakes cause movements called vibrations. These vibrations change speeds and directions when they go into different layers of the Earth. Scientists can study these vibrations. They use a tool called a seismograph that is attached to the rock of the crust. The information can help scientists learn the depth and properties of each layer.

Finally, scientists perform laboratory experiments to learn about Earth's layers. They test how heat and pressure change materials they think are found inside Earth.

© Pearson Education, Inc. 5

Lesson 1 Checkpoint

1. What are Earth's layers?

_____

_____

_____

_____

2. How does the mantle material get energy to move in convection currents?

_____

_____

3. Make a diagram of Earth's layers. On the diagram label and describe the crust, mantle, inner core, outer core, and lithosphere.

4. How are earthquake vibrations used to study Earth's layers?

_____

_____

_____

5. ⊙ **Summarize** What is the main idea of this lesson? Include three details.

_____

_____

_____

© Pearson Education, Inc. 5

Lesson 2: What causes earthquakes and volcanoes?

Vocabulary

plate a section of the lithosphere

Earth's Plates

The lithosphere covers all of Earth like a thin shell. But it is not a solid piece of material. The lithosphere is broken up into small and large **plates.** Some plates are larger than continents. The edges of a plate are called plate boundaries. Plates meet at plate boundaries.

Earth's plates slowly move. Some plates move slower than 1 centimeter per year, but others move as fast as 24 centimeters per year. Plates might move together, pull apart from each other, or move past each other. These movements can cause big changes on Earth's surface. Some of these changes happen very slowly. For example, mountains and valleys can form over long periods of time. Other changes happen quickly during earthquakes.

Gravity pulls plates down toward the mantle. Convection currents in the mantle also push and pull on the plates.

There are three kinds of plate boundaries. A converging boundary is when two plates collide. Mountains can form when one plate folds, tilts, and lifts up.

A spreading plate boundary forms when two plates move apart from each other. An example of this is on the floor of the ocean. As the plates spread, the ocean becomes wider.

A sliding plate boundary forms when two plates move past each other in opposite directions. One plate may move northward while another plate moves southward.

Earthquakes

Earthquakes happen at faults. A fault is a crack in the crust. The rock around a fault has moved or shifted. Faults can form almost anywhere.

Most earthquakes occur at faults near plate boundaries. The plates lock in place. Then the plates jerk into a new position. This sudden movement causes an earthquake. Plate movements usually happen far below ground. The place where the plates slip is called a focus. The place on Earth's surface above the focus is called the epicenter.

Earthquakes are quick, destructive forces. They can cause landslides. A landslide is the downhill movement of large amounts of rock and soil. Earthquakes under the ocean can cause tsunamis. Tsunamis are giant waves that can cause destruction when they crash into a coastline.

Volcanoes

Most volcanoes form near colliding plate boundaries. Rock partially melts to make magma as one plate moves below another plate. Lava is melted rock on Earth's surface and through a hole called a vent. Water vapor and carbon dioxide are often mixed with the lava. Trapped gases can have enough pressure to blow apart the side of a volcano. Trapped gases also push lava high into the air.

Volcanoes can also form from the ocean floor. These can be constructive forces that build new features. Volcanoes can form islands when they reach the surface of the water.

© Pearson Education, Inc. 5

Lesson 2 Checkpoint

1. How do mountains form at plate boundaries?

_____

_____

2. How are earthquakes, landslides, tsunamis, and plates all related?

_____

_____

_____

_____

3. Name and describe the three types of plate boundaries.

_____

_____

_____

_____

4. How do volcanoes and volcanic islands form?

_____

_____

5. Use the Internet or library resources to write a report about how to be safe during an earthquake. Include in your report how technologies make buildings more safe to be in during an earthquake.

Lesson 3: What is weathering?

Vocabulary

mechanical weathering the breaking of rock into smaller pieces by forces due to gravity, ice, plant roots, or other forces

chemical weathering the changing of materials in a rock by chemical processes

Weathering and Soil

Weathering is a slow process. Weathering breaks rocks into small pieces. These pieces are called sediments. There are two kinds of weathering: mechanical weathering and chemical weathering.

Water can freeze in the cracks of rocks. Water expands when it freezes. This causes rocks to split. This kind of **mechanical weathering** is called ice wedging.

Changes in pressure can cause rocks to break. Wind or water can remove large amounts of dirt from a mountainside. As a result, rocks in the mountain are under less pressure. These rocks expand at different speeds. This causes cracks to form in the rock. Over time, the cracks grow larger. Gravity pulls pieces of rock to the bottom of the mountain. Water can move into the cracks and freeze when it becomes cold.

Plant roots can also grow in the cracks of a rock. In warm, wet conditions, the roots push the rock apart. Roots break soft rocks like sandstone more quickly than hard rocks like granite. Mechanical weathering happens to different rocks at different rates.

In **chemical weathering** rocks are broken down by the actions of chemicals. Raindrops can dissolve the material in some rocks. Raindrops take in carbon dioxide from the air and make a chemical called carbonic acid. Raindrops soak into the soil down to the rock. The acid in the water dissolves parts of the rocks. This can form caves.

Chemical weathering can also be caused by fungi and other organisms. These organisms give off chemicals that can change rocks.

Like mechanical weathering, chemical weathering affects some rocks faster than others. For example, limestone weathers more quickly than granite. Different climates cause chemical weathering to happen at different rates. Both kinds of weathering happen faster in places that receive a lot of rain.

Mechanical weathering and chemical weathering help make soil. Soil is a mixture of sediment, decayed material, gases from air, and water.

There are many kinds of soil. They can be red, brown, black, or gray. The color of the soil depends on the materials in the soil.

The size of a soil's sediments controls its texture. Some soil is made of very small sediments, like clay. These soils feel smooth. Water does not pass through these soils easily. Other soils are made of larger sediments, like sand. Sandy soils feel rough or gritty. Sandy soils let water pass through easily.

There are three layers of soil. Topsoil, the top layer of soil, has a large amount of decayed material in it. Decayed materials help plants grow. Subsoil is the second layer of soil. It is usually a different color than topsoil and has less decayed material in it. But subsoil does contain many minerals. Bedrock, the third layer of soil, is almost solid rock. Water can get into the cracks in bedrock and can weather bedrock into smaller pieces. These pieces can become sediments in the soil.

© Pearson Education, Inc. **5**

Lesson 3 Checkpoint

1. What are two ways that mechanical weathering changes rocks?

   _____

   _____

2. How are mechanical and chemical weathering alike? How are they different?

   _____

   _____

   _____

3. Two identical statues are placed outside. One is made of limestone and one is made of granite. Which statue will weather more slowly?

   _____

   _____

4. Describe the layers of soil and how soil is made.

   _____

   _____

   _____

Lesson 4: What is erosion?

Erosion and Deposition

Erosion is the movement of materials away from one place. It is a destructive process. Deposition is the placing of the materials in a new place. Deposition is a constructive process. Erosion and deposition together create valleys, deltas, and sand dunes.

Gravity is the main force causing erosion. Gravity pulls rocks and dirt downhill. This is called a landslide. A landslide is one kind of erosion.

Gravity also causes rivers to flow. Rivers pick up and carry sediment as they flow downhill. The sediment can erode riverbeds and form deep canyons.

Rivers also cause deposition. A river flows much slower when it meets an ocean. This causes the river to deposit heavy sediment like gravel and sand. The sediment create a delta.

Glaciers are big bodies of ice that can cause erosion. Gravity pulls glaciers down along a valley. Rocks beneath the glaciers are broken down into sediment. The glacier moves the sediment downhill. This can make the bottom of a valley more U-shaped over time.

Waves are a source of erosion and deposition. Waves from storms or tides crash against rocks along the coastline. The rocks break. Sand and gravel in the waves acts like sandpaper. They wear down the rocks even more. This is how some of the sand on beaches is created.

Not all parts of a shoreline are eroded at the same rate. Harbors and inlets form when some areas erode more quickly than others. A harbor is an area that is protected from ocean waves. Waves can make caves when parts of a cliff erode more quickly than other parts of the cliff.

Waves push sand when they hit beaches. A spit is a narrow piece of sandy land. A baymouth bar is like a spit. But it forms across a bay. Barrier islands form along coastlines. Erosion can move barrier islands.

The wind can move dust, dirt, or sand from one place to another. This dust and sand can blow against a rock. Tiny bits of the rock might break off and blow away. This is erosion.

The wind deposits large, loose amounts of sand to create sand dunes. Wind pushes sand up one side. This sand will move over the edge of the dune's top. The sand will pile up until gravity pulls it down. This creates a steeper slope than the one that faces the wind.

Winds can move a sand dune. The wind will pick up sand from one side of the dune and deposit it on the other side. This causes the dune to slowly move in the direction of the wind.

Wind erosion can cause problems on farms. If bare, plowed fields become very dry, the wind can blow the topsoil off the fields. Topsoil is the best kind of soil for growing crops. It cannot be quickly replaced.

Farmers try to prevent wind erosion by planting trees along the edges of fields to block some of the wind.

© Pearson Education, Inc. 5

Lesson 4 Checkpoint

1. Suppose sand, gravel, and clay are being carried by a river. As the water enters a lake and slows down, in what order will these sediments settle out of the water? Explain why they settle out in this order.

_____

_____

2. Describe how waves, currents, tides, and storms affect the geological features of the ocean shore (beaches, barrier islands, inlets, and harbors).

_____

_____

_____

3. Define erosion, and tell how gravity works with water, ice, and wind to cause erosion.

_____

_____

_____

4. How does a delta form?

_____

_____

5. How do sand dunes form? Why is one side of a dune different than the other side?

_____

_____

Lesson 5: How are minerals identified?

Properties of Minerals

To a scientist, a mineral is a natural solid whose particles make a pattern. Soil and rocks are made of minerals. There are many different minerals. However, only a few dozen minerals make up most of the rocks on Earth.

Every mineral has certain properties. Minerals can give off a sweet, earthy smell, or a rotten egg smell. Some minerals make tiny bubbles when they touch chemicals called acids. Scientists use the following properties to identify minerals.

- Hardness: Some minerals are harder than others. The Mohs scale is used to tell how hard a mineral is. The scale rates the hardness of minerals from 1 to 10. Talc is the softest mineral. It has a hardness of 1. Diamonds are the hardest minerals. They have a hardness of 10.

- Magnetism: Some minerals have magnetic properties. Pyrrhotite and magnetite are minerals that are strongly magnetic.

- Luster: Luster is the way a mineral's surface reflects light. A mineral's luster can be glassy, earthy, metallic, waxy, silky, or pearly.

- Shape: Not all minerals have specific shapes. But pyrite, for example, is shaped like cubes. A mineral's shape will cause the mineral to break in specific patterns.

- Streak: Scientists rub minerals on a hard, rough, white surface. This makes a powder. The color of the powder is a mineral's streak. A mineral's streak is usually different from the mineral's outside color.

- Texture: Texture is how a mineral feels. A mineral's texture might be sandy, sticky, smooth, or powdery.

Using Properties to Identify Minerals

Scientists record the properties of unknown minerals. Then they compare these observations to minerals they have already studied.

Look at the chart on page 284 in your textbook. This chart shows the properties of some known minerals. Identify the minerals on page 285 in your textbook by comparing them to the chart.

Lesson 5 Checkpoint

1. What properties are used to identify minerals?

_____

_____

_____

_____

2. What is a mineral?

_____

_____

3. How is a mineral's streak determined?

_____

_____

_____

Lesson 6: How are rocks classified?

Vocabulary

igneous rocks that form when melted rock cools and hardens

sedimentary rocks that form when layers of materials and rock particles settle on top of each other and then harden

metamorphic rocks that form when solid rock is squeezed and heated to a very high temperatures

Igneous Rocks

There are three general kinds of rocks: igneous, sedimentary, and metamorphic. Each kind of rock is formed in a different way.

Igneous rocks form when melted rock cools and hardens. Mineral crystals form as this hot rock cools. Large crystals form when the rock cools slowly. Granite has large crystals. Small crystals form when the rock cools quickly. Basalt has small crystals.

Sedimentary Rocks

Sedimentary rocks form when layers of materials and sediments settle on top of each other. These sediments harden. Natural chemicals act like cement and hold the sediments together. Sandstone and conglomerate are examples of sedimentary rocks.

Fossils often form in sedimentary rock. Scientists study the rock around the fossil. They look at the size and shape of the rock's sand grains. Scientists try to find which minerals make up the sand grains. This information gives us clues about the environment when the organism was living.

Metamorphic Rocks

Certain conditions are necessary for **metamorphic** rock to form. Solid rock must be squeezed and heated to high temperatures. This causes rock particles to form a new pattern. The properties of the rock change and new minerals may form. This creates metamorphic rock.

The Rock Cycle

Rocks can change from one kind to another in the rock cycle. An igneous rock could become a metamorphic rock thousands of years from now. Or rocks can stay the same for millions of years. Look at the diagram of the rock cycle on pages 288–289 in your textbook. The diagram shows three classes of rock: igneous, sedimentary, and metamorphic rock. The diagram shows processes that form them:

- Heat and pressure can change igneous rocks into metamorphic rocks.
- Cooling can change metamorphic rocks into igneous rocks.
- Weathering can change metamorphic or igneous rocks to sedimentary rocks.

Relative Ages of Rocks

Rock layers at Earth's surface are younger than rock layers below them. Events like earthquakes and volcanoes can make these layers bend or turn over.

Scientists study rock layers to understand past events. Bent or broken layers of rock show scientists that something moved these layers after they were made.

Scientists use rock layers to determine the age of fossils. Fossils in upper rock layers are considered younger than fossils in lower layers.

Lesson 6 Checkpoint

1. Why do some igneous rocks have larger crystals than others?

_____

_____

2. Draw a diagram of the rock cycle. Label and describe each class of rock and the processes that form each.

3. What conditions are necessary in order for metamorphic rock to form?

_____

_____

4. How are sedimentary rock layers used by scientists to learn about the past?

_____

_____

_____

5. 🎯 **Summarize** List the four most important ideas you learned in this lesson.

_____

_____

_____

_____

Use with pp. 303–305

Lesson 1: What are nonrenewable energy resources?

Vocabulary

resource a supply that will meet a need for materials or energy

renewable resource a resource that can be replaced

nonrenewable resource a resource that either cannot be replaced at all or cannot be replaced as fast as we use it

fossil fuels energy resource made from the remains of organisms

Types of Resources

A **resource** can be used for materials or energy. A **renewable resource** can be replaced. Trees are a renewable resource. People can cut down trees and plant new trees. The new tree replaces the old tree.

Some **nonrenewable resources** can never be replaced. Other nonrenewable resources cannot be replaced as quickly as we use them.

Coal is a nonrenewable resource that forms from plants. Plants in swampy places use energy from sunlight to grow. Layers of dead plants can build up and form a material called peat. In time, peat gets buried. It slowly changes into soft coal. Then it changes into hard coal.

Coal is a fuel. It can be burned to make heat or energy. The energy in coal was once sunlight energy that plants used.

Petroleum and natural gas are also fuels. Most scientists think natural gas and petroleum form in a way similar to coal. However, they did not begin as plants. They began as small sea organisms. So, crude oil and natural gas are called **fossil fuels.**

Oil and Natural Gas

Drills make deep holes in Earth's surface to find oil. Crude oil can be on land or under the ocean floor. Natural gas is often found near crude oil. Natural gas can be pumped into pipelines that carry it to tanks until it is needed.

Crude oil can be used to make gasoline and other fuels. These fuels run machines. Cars, trucks, trains, and ships burn fuel. Some power plants burn fuel to make electricity. Farms use tractors that burn fuel.

Crude oil can be used to make other products too. It is used to make asphalt, plastic, grease, and wax.

Advantages and Disadvantages

Fossil fuels have many advantages over other energy sources. Coal and oil are easy to store and move. Large amounts of energy come from fossil fuels. It is harder to get the same amount of energy from other energy sources.

But fossil fuels also have disadvantages. The supply of fossil fuels is limited. Burning coal and oil also causes air pollution. Oil can cause water pollution. There is the danger of oil spills when the boats have accidents. Plants and animals are harmed when oil spills into water.

Careful planning can help people use fossil fuels wisely. For example, many new cars can travel farther with less fuel and cause less pollution.

Lesson 1 Checkpoint

1. Where does the energy of coal originally come from?

_____

2. How does coal form?

_____

_____

_____

3. What are the problems and benefits of using nonrenewable energy sources?

_____

_____

_____

_____

4. **Main Idea and Details** What is the main idea of the third paragraph on page 304 of your textbook?

_____

_____

Lesson 2: What are other energy resources?

Vocabulary

solar energy energy from sunlight

hydroelectric making electricity from the energy of flowing water

geothermal energy from the high temperatures inside the Earth

biomass material that was recently alive

Solar Energy

You read that fossil fuels have some disadvantages. Fossil fuels are polluting and nonrenewable. So, it is important to find more renewable energy sources that are nonpolluting.

Solar energy is energy from sunlight. Solar cells use sunlight to make electricity. People use sunlight to heat water. Sunlight is also used to heat air in buildings.

Solar energy is renewable. It does not pollute the environment. But we cannot get solar energy at night or on cloudy days. Changing solar energy into electricity is expensive. Factories that make solar cells can also create dangerous wastes.

Wind Energy

Windmills have been used to grind grain and pump water for many years. Wind turbines are used to change wind energy into electricity and do not cause pollution. But wind turbines also have some disadvantages. Wind does not blow all the time. Birds can die if they fly into the turbines.

Moving Water

Hydroelectric power plants use moving water to make electricity. These plants are usually built in dams. Parts of generators spin as water moves through the dam. As they spin, they make electricity.

Hydroelectric plants do not use fuel to make electricity. They do not create pollution. But they can only be built near moving water. The area also has to have a place where a lake can form behind a dam. These lakes flood animal and plant habitats. The dams can also harm fish.

Nuclear Energy

Nuclear power uses hot uranium to make steam. The steam makes electricity. Nuclear power plants use less fuel than power plants that use coal or oil. Also, nuclear power plants do not produce smoke. But nuclear power plants are expensive to build. They make harmful wastes. Also, uranium is a rare metal and a nonrenewable energy source.

Geothermal Energy

Geothermal energy is made from high temperatures inside the Earth. One way this energy is used is to pour water down deep holes into hot rock. The hot rock heats the water. Hot water or steam rushes to the surface. This is used to make electricity.

Geothermal energy can make electricity all day and all night. It can be used all year long. But geothermal energy cannot be made in many places. The steam can also cause pollution.

Energy of Biomass

Biomass is burned to make electricity. **Biomass** is material that was recently alive. Biomass is found in garbage. We will always have garbage. This means biomass is renewable. Burning biomass does make air pollution, though.

© Pearson Education, Inc. 5

Lesson 2 Checkpoint

1. Why do we need to improve sources of energy that are not fossil fuels?

   _____

   _____

2. What are the environmental advantages and disadvantages of wind turbines?

   _____

   _____

3. What are the good and bad effects of building dams to run hydroelectric power plants?

   _____

   _____

4. Describe two ways that people use energy from the Sun. What are the advantages and disadvantages of getting energy in these ways?

   _____

   _____

5. What kind of energy uses uranium as a fuel? What are the advantages and disadvantages of getting energy in this way?

   _____

   _____

6. How do people use geothermal energy?

   _____

   _____

Use with pp. 314–317

Lesson 3: What are other resources?

Mineral Resources

Minerals are resources such as gold, iron, copper, and salt. Gold and silver are hard to find. Salt and iron are easy to find. Workers often dig for these nonliving materials in mines. Towns often grow where minerals are mined.

Minerals have many uses. Iron is a useful and inexpensive metal. Iron can be mixed with other minerals. Steel is made of iron and carbon. We use steel to make cars and buildings.

Gypsum is a white material from rocks. We use it in plaster and paint. Mica is another mineral we use in paint.

Gravel is made of small pieces of rocks and sand. Many roads are made of gravel. Other roads are made of gravel covered with asphalt or concrete. Concrete is made of gravel, sand, water, and cement.

Some Uses of Iron Ore

All minerals are nonrenewable. But Earth has large amounts of some minerals, such as iron. Copper, lead, and zinc are much more limited.

Mining for minerals changes the land. Mining changes the habitats of plants and animals. Mining also causes air and water pollution. Some ways of mining leave large holes in the land and can lead to mud slides and soil erosion.

Water, Soil, and Air

Water, soil, and air are important resources because they fill a need. We need water, soil, and air for many reasons.

- Air: You need air to stay alive. Air fills your lungs. It gives your body oxygen. Nitrogen in the air makes many fertilizers that farmers use for their plants. Air can become polluted from volcanoes and forest fires. Burning fuels also pollute the air. Air pollution can cause health problems for people and animals.
- Soil: Plants need soil to stay alive. Soil has minerals and nutrients plants need. Soil can be polluted with chemicals. Growing too many crops can damage soil. Wind and water can also erode soil.
- Water: People, plants, and animals need water to stay alive. People also use water to bathe, cook, and wash. Water is used to grow food and make electricity.

Pollution can enter water when people dump wastes into it. Air pollution can get into rain as it falls to the ground. Water pollution can harm plants, animals, and buildings.

Air, soil, and water are partly renewable. Water can be recycled in the water cycle. Air pollution slowly settles out of the air. New soil is always being made. But these processes take a very long time. So we must take care of these resources every day.

Lesson 3 Checkpoint

1. How does the location of towns and cities relate to the Earth's resources?

_____

_____

2. Explain why it is necessary to carefully maintain a resource even if it is renewable.

_____

_____

_____

3. Why are soil, water, and air considered to be resources?

_____

_____

Lesson 4: Can resources be conserved?

Repairing Soil, Water, and Air

The use of machines has caused air, soil, and water pollution. Pollution has had a major effect on the environment. Some towns have become so polluted that people had to leave. The pollution was dangerous to people's health. Removing pollution is very expensive.

You cannot always see pollution in the environment. Scientists monitor pollution in the air, soil, and water. *Monitor* means "to check". Monitoring pollution can also help people find out where pollution is coming from, and keep it from increasing.

Conservation Laws

There are laws to protect the natural resources. For example, businesses in many areas have to plant new trees to replace trees they cut down. Some factories must clean the lands they pollute. Other laws have set aside land to be used as national parks. These parks protect environments.

Using Less and Reusing Resources

Both large companies and each person can help protect Earth's resources by using less of them. Resources can be saved in many ways. You can turn off lights you are not using. Power plants can burn less fuel when you use less electricity. This reduces air pollution too.

Some companies are saving resources by using less material to make the same product. For example, aluminum cans are thinner now than they were in the past.

People and businesses can also reuse resources. You can reuse the back of paper. Some businesses help people reuse things by selling used goods. Some companies reuse old computer parts. Old tires can be reused to make playground surfaces.

Recycling

Another way to save resources is to recycle. Recycling is changing something so it can be used again. Glass can be recycled. First, it is ground up. Then the glass is melted to make new bottles and jars. Glass can also be used to pave roads.

Paper can also be recycled. The paper is soaked in water and chemicals. It becomes a soft, wet pulp. Then the pulp is pushed through screens to remove objects mixed with the paper. Next, ink is taken out of the pulp. Finally, the clean pulp is pressed and dried to make new paper.

Plastics can be recycled too. Look at the pictures on page 320 in your textbook. These pictures show how plastic is recycled.

Recycling can save materials. It can also save energy. For example, there is a large supply of aluminum in the Earth. But it takes less energy to recycle aluminum than it does to get aluminum from a mine.

You can help save resources by recycling at home and at school. Collect paper, cans, plastics, and glass. Ask an adult to help you get these resources to a recycling center.

© Pearson Education, Inc. 5

Lesson 4 Checkpoint

1. Why is it important to monitor air and water?

_____
_____
_____

2. Explain why and how people maintain natural resources.

_____
_____
_____

3. Demonstrate how people and companies can use technology to reduce the production of waste and reduce the use of resources. How do these actions affect the environment?

_____
_____
_____
_____

4. Look around your classroom. Identify and classify materials that can be recycled.

_____
_____

Lesson 1: What are properties of matter?

Vocabulary

elements the basic building blocks of matter

Elements

Elements are basic kinds of matter. They combine to form other kinds of matter. There are more than 100 elements.

Only a few pure elements are found in nature. Gold is a pure element. However, most elements combine to form things around us. For example, rust is made of iron and oxygen.

Each element has its own chemical and physical properties. Chemical properties tell how a material changes into other materials. Physical properties tell an object's color, smell, density, texture, and hardness.

Weight, Mass, and Volume

Weight is a measure of the pull of gravity on an object. Weight changes when the pull of gravity changes. Gravity is not the same everywhere on Earth. The pull of gravity is a little smaller at the top of a mountain. So an object's weight is less at the top of a mountain. You can measure weight with a spring scale by attaching an object to a spring. Measure how much the spring stretches or tightens.

Mass is the amount of matter in an object. The amount of mass affects the weight of an object. But mass does not change with gravity. Moving an object to the top of a mountain does not change an object's mass. You can measure mass with a balance. Place an object on one side of the balance and put objects with known masses on the other side. The weights are equal when the two sides balance. Mass is measured in grams, milligrams, or kilograms.

Volume is the amount of space that an object takes up. Volume is measured in cubic units. For example, you can find the volume of a box. Measure and multiply the box's length, width, and height.

A cylinder is used to measure the volume of a liquid. Lines on the side of the cylinder tell you the volume.

Properties of Objects and Materials

There is a difference between an object's properties and a material's properties. What are the physical properties of the gold bar on page 344 in your textbook? The bar's shape is rectangular. The bar has a certain size and volume. But these properties will change if you cut or crush the bar.

However, the gold's properties do not change when you cut or crush the bar because it is a material. Gold's density is the same no matter what shape it has. Other material properties include color, hardness, and texture.

Density and Buoyancy

Density is the amount of matter in a given volume. To find density, divide an object's mass by its volume. Density is a physical property of a material.

Another important property is buoyancy. An object is buoyant if it floats in liquid. An object will float if its density is less than the liquid's density. It will sink if its density is greater than the liquid's density. Look at the density chart on page 346 in your textbook. Notice that the density of the beeswax is less than that of water. This means that beeswax floats in water. Find olive oil on the chart. The density of the beeswax is greater than the density of the olive oil. Beeswax sinks in olive oil.

Lesson 1 Checkpoint

1. How many elements are there? Are things around us usually made of pure elements or combinations of elements?

_____

_____

2. Is volume a property of an object, or the matter that makes it up?

_____

3. If you had two equally sized objects, how could you tell which one is more dense?

_____

_____

4. Suppose you had a material that is listed in the density table on page 346 of your textbook. It floats in water but sinks in olive oil. What is the material? How do you know?

_____

_____

Lesson 2: How do atoms combine?

Vocabulary

atom smallest particle of an element with the properties of the element

neutron part of an atom's center that has no electrical charge

proton part of an atom's center that has a positive electrical charge

electron part of an atom that has a negative electrical charge

compound a type of matter made of a combination of elements

Atoms

Every element is made of tiny atoms. Atoms of one element are different from atoms of another element. Every **atom** has properties that decide how the element can combine with other atoms.

An atom usually has neutrons and protons. **Electrons** move around the protons and neutrons. Electrons may join or leave atoms. **Protons** have a positive electrical charge. Electrons have a negative charge. **Neutrons** have no charge.

The periodic table on pages 348–349 of your textbook shows all of the elements. The number above the letter shows how many protons are in the atoms of the element. For example, chlorine atoms have 17 protons and fluorine atoms have 9 protons.

The order of the elements in the table is important. The elements are put in rows, based on the number of protons each element has. The elements in each column share chemical properties.

Compounds

A **compound** is a type of matter made of more than one element. Most things are compounds. The smallest part of a compound is a molecule which is made of two or more atoms bonded together.

The properties of a compound are different from the properties of its elements. For example, sugar is made of carbon, hydrogen, and oxygen. These elements are not sweet in their pure forms.

Some compounds form when atoms share electrons. The electrons bond these atoms together. Every compound has a name and a formula. The numbers in the formula show how many atoms of each element are in the compound. For example, the formula for water is H_2O. The H stands for hydrogen. The 2 after the H shows that a water molecule has 2 hydrogen atoms. The O stands for oxygen. There is no number after the O because there is only 1 oxygen atom in a water molecule.

Images of Molecules

Atoms and molecules are so small that you cannot see them with a microscope. Scientists use special technology to make images of atoms and molecules that can be drawn on a computer screen.

Salts

Salts are compounds whose molecules are held together by opposite charges. The properties of a salt are different from its elements. Table salt is made of sodium and chlorine. These elements can be dangerous in their pure forms when particles with an electrical charge form certain patterns.

© Pearson Education, Inc. 5

Lesson 2 Checkpoint

1. Describe the periodic table and how it is organized.

_____

_____

2. 🎯 **Predict** If atoms of chlorine and fluorine easily take on 1 additional electron, use the table on pages 348–349 in your textbook to predict which other kinds of atoms will also have this chemical property. Write their names.

_____

_____

3. In a formula for a compound, what do the numbers tell you?

_____

_____

4. Compare table salt with glucose.

_____

_____

5. Write a paragraph that tells how the words *matter, element, atom, crystal, compound,* and *molecule* relate.

_____

_____

_____

6. 🎯 **Predict** Suppose a large atom bonds with a small atom. Predict whether the properties of the new molecule will be the same as the large atom, the same as the small atom, or different from both atoms.

_____

_____

Lesson 3: How do phase changes occur?

Solids and Liquids

There are three phases of matter. They are solid, liquid, and gas. Every material can form a solid, a liquid, or a gas. The shape and movement of a material's particles determines its phase or state. A material's phase is a physical property.

A solid has a definite shape and volume. The particles in a solid move back and forth quickly. The particles in most solids are very close together.

A solid melts when it heats up. This means a solid changes into a liquid. A liquid's particles can move past one another. Therefore, liquids do not have their own shape. They take the shape of their container. The particles in a liquid stay close together. Liquids have an exact volume.

A liquid can cool and freeze. This makes the liquid's particles slow down. They begin to move in place. The freezing point is the temperature at which a liquid freezes. The melting point is the temperature at which a solid melts. The freezing point and melting point are the same temperature. For example, water freezes at 0°C. Ice melts when its temperature rises above 0°C.

Different materials have different freezing points. A material's freezing point is a physical property. A material's freezing point does not change unless the material changes. For example, water has a freezing point of 0°C. The freezing point will be lower if salt is added to the water.

Materials change size when they change temperatures. A material's particles move faster when the material heats up. Particles that move faster usually have more space between them. This space causes the material to get larger.

Materials can become smaller when they cool. The particles in colder material move more slowly. There is less space between them. But particles never get cold enough to stop moving.

Gases

Gases do not have a definite shape or volume. Gas particles are far apart.

Particles can leave a liquid and become a gas. This is called evaporation. Particles evaporate if they are at the top of a liquid and move upward.

Particles can evaporate throughout a liquid if the temperature is high enough. Gas particles move quickly upward through the liquid. They form bubbles of gas under the surface of the liquid. The boiling point of a liquid is the temperature at which the liquid turns into gas bubbles. Every liquid has a boiling point. It is a physical property of a liquid. Different liquids have different boiling points.

Condensation takes place when a gas turns into a liquid. This happens when gas particles touch something cold. The gas particles cool and slow down. The cold object attracts and traps more gas particles. The trapped particles form a drop of liquid. Clouds in the sky and dew on the ground are formed by condensation.

Lesson 3 Checkpoint

1. Why do materials change size when they change temperature?

_____

_____

2. Compare the motion and spacing of particles as a material cools from a gas to a liquid and then to a solid phase. Do particles ever stop moving?

_____

_____

3. Define and compare boiling points, melting points, and freezing points.

_____

_____

Lesson 4: What are mixtures and solutions?

Vocabulary

saturated containing all the solute that can be dissolved without changing the temperature

concentrated having so much solute that it is relatively close to being saturated

dilute being far from saturated

Mixtures

A mixture is different from a compound. Different elements bond together to form a compound. In a mixture, different materials are placed together but they do not bond. Usually, the different materials keep their own properties. For example, suppose that you put salt and pepper together to form a mixture. The salt and pepper do not change their flavors or colors.

Separating a Mixture

The materials in a simple mixture have different properties. You can use these properties to separate the materials. Pretend you mix small iron pieces with sand. You could use a magnet to separate the mixture. The magnet will attract the iron. The magnet will not attract the sand.

Some metals are elements, such as gold, silver, copper, iron, and nickel. Many metals are mixtures of elements. Steel is a mixture of iron and carbon. Brass is a mixture of copper and zinc. These mixtures are called alloys.

Solutions

What happens if you mix dirt with water? The dirt will slowly fall to the bottom. What happens when you mix sugar with water? The sugar will not fall to the bottom. Sugar and water make a kind of mixture called a solution.

The materials in a solution spread out evenly. They do not fall to the bottom. There are two parts to a solution. The solute is the material that spreads out, or dissolves. Sugar is the solute in sugar water. The solvent is the material in which the solute dissolves. Water is the solvent in sugar water. Water can be a solvent in many solutions. It is called a universal solvent.

What happens when a solute dissolves? Solute particles spread throughout the solvent. Heating and stirring can make a solute dissolve more quickly. Breaking a solid solute into smaller pieces also helps it dissolve faster.

In many solutions, a solid dissolves in a liquid. Two liquids can also make a solution. A gas can also dissolve in a liquid.

Solubility is a physical property. Solubility is how much of a substance can be dissolved by a solvent at a certain temperature or pressure. Solubility increases when temperature increases. For example, hot water can hold more salt than cold water.

Solutions can be saturated, concentrated, or diluted. A **saturated** solution has all the solute that can be dissolved without changing the temperature. The solute will not dissolve if you add more of it to a saturated solution. A **concentrated** solution has a lot of solute. It is close to being saturated. A **dilute** solution has very little solute. It is far from saturated.

Many materials will not form solutions. For example, pepper will not dissolve in water.

© Pearson Education, Inc. 5

Lesson 4 Checkpoint

1. Name 5 metals that are pure elements and 3 that are mixtures.

_____

_____

2. Could a mixture of pepper and water also be called a solution?
   Could a mixture of salt and water also be called a solution? Explain
   your answers.

_____

_____

3. How can you cause more solid solute be dissolved in a liquid?

_____

_____

Lesson 1: What are chemical changes?

Vocabulary

physical change a change in which the material keeps its identify

chemical change a change in which one substance or kind of matter changes into another completely different kind of matter with different properties

combustion a very quick chemical process that gives off energy, such as what takes place during burning

Physical and Chemical Changes

There are two ways that matter can change. Matter can undergo physical changes and chemical changes. When a **physical change** happens, the substance keeps its identity. The material itself does not change. Cutting a piece of wood is a physical change. But the wood is still wood. Physical changes can change the material's size, shape, or position. Physical changes can also change the phase of matter. For example, rain can freeze and become sleet. Rain and sleet are different phases of the same material: water.

When a **chemical change** happens, the materials themselves change. When you burn wood, it changes into ash and smoke. These are different materials. Rust is a chemical change. Iron changes when it is put in ocean water for a long time. The surface of an iron ship changes into a new material: iron oxide. Iron oxide is another name for rust. Iron oxide has different chemical and physical properties than iron.

Evidence of Chemical Change

When a chemical change takes place, atoms rearrange themselves. They form different kinds of matter. Sometimes a chemical change is easy to see. You might see a change in color. When iron rusts, it becomes iron oxide. Iron oxide has a different color. You can see this chemical change easily.

In other chemical changes, a gas forms. An antacid tablet creates a chemical change. When you drop the tablet in water, it bubbles. The bubbles are carbon dioxide gas.

In other chemical changes, a solid may form. Look at the pictures on pages 376–377 in your textbook. A copper tree is placed into a liquid. A chemical change happens. Crystals form on the wire. The crystals are new solids. They are evidence of a chemical change.

Chemical Changes and Energy Changes

In some chemical changes, the bonds between atoms change. Old bonds break and new bonds form. Breaking and forming bonds involves energy. Energy is taken in or given off. In some chemical changes, you can see the energy changes. Burning is a very fast chemical change called **combustion.** When you burn a log, the log gives off energy. We see this energy as light and feel it as heat. Other chemical changes may produce electric energy.

Lesson 1 Checkpoint

1. What is the difference between a chemical change and a physical change?

_____

_____

2. List three types of evidence of chemical change.

_____

_____

_____

3. Compare the second and third pictures of the copper tree experiment on pages 376 and 377 of your textbook. Aside from the forming of solid crystals, what other evidence of chemical change in the liquid do you see?

_____

_____

4. 🎯 **Draw Conclusions** When you cook an egg, do you think a chemical change occurs? Why or why not?

_____

_____

Lesson 2: What are some kinds of chemical reactions?

Vocabulary

> **reactant** a substance used in a chemical reaction
>
> **product** a substance made during a chemical reaction
>
> **chemical equation** a "sentence" that shows what happens during a chemical reaction

Chemical Equations

When a chemical reaction takes place, materials change into other materials. The new materials have different chemical and physical properties. The **reactants** are the materials at the beginning of the chemical reaction. The **products** are the materials that are made during a chemical reaction. The reactants change. They become the products.

A **chemical equation** shows what happens in a chemical reaction. The left side of the equation shows the reactants. The right side of the equation shows the products. There is an arrow between the two sides. To read a chemical equation, you can say "makes" for the arrow.

The picture on page 378 in your textbook shows electricity flowing in water. The electricity causes a chemical change. The water molecules change into hydrogen and oxygen gases. You can write a chemical equation to describe this chemical reaction:

Water⟶Hydrogen + Oxygen

You can read this equation: "Water makes hydrogen and oxygen gases."

Magnesium is a gray metal. At high temperatures, it reacts with oxygen in the air. It burns with a bright white glow. Then a white powder forms. This powder is magnesium oxide.

Magnesium + Oxygen⟶Magnesium Oxide

Matter Is Always Conserved

A chemical reaction never changes the amount of matter. The Law of Conservation says that matter cannot be created or destroyed by a chemical reaction. The two sides of a chemical equation always have the same mass.

If you make a cake, you mix ingredients together. A chemical reaction happens when you bake the cake. But the amount of matter stays the same. The mass of the ingredients equals the mass of the baked cake plus gases and water vapor that escaped during baking.

Types of Chemical Reactions

Three important kinds of chemical reactions are decomposition, combination, and replacement.

- Decomposition reaction: When compounds break apart to form smaller compounds or elements. For example, water molecules split apart to form hydrogen and oxygen.
- Combination reaction: When elements or compounds come together to form new compounds. If iron and sulfur come together, they form iron sulfide.
- Replacement reaction: When one or more compounds break apart, the parts switch places. Think of a burning candle. Wax can be made of carbon and hydrogen. When the wax burns, the wax molecules and oxygen molecules break apart. They rejoin in new compounds such as carbon dioxide and water.

© Pearson Education, Inc. 5

Lesson 2 Checkpoint

1. What do chemical equations show?

_____

_____

2. Describe three kinds of chemical reactions.

_____

_____

_____

3. In the chemical reaction described on page 379 of your textbook, magnesium reacts with oxygen gas. What kind of chemical reaction is this? Explain.

_____

_____

_____

Lesson 3: How are chemical properties used?

Separating Mixtures

Physical changes can separate some mixtures. If you mix salt and pepper together, you can use their physical properties to separate them.

Substances may have different chemical properties that can be used to separate them from each other. For example, some scientists use chemical properties to separate limestone from fossils. Limestone can be dissolved by vinegar. The fossil is made of another kind of rock with different chemical properties. Vinegar does not affect the fossil so it is a good chemical to use to separate fossils from rock.

Separating Metals from Ores

Ores are rocks that contain metals and other materials. People use chemistry to separate the metals from the other materials. For example, iron ore contains iron oxide. You can heat the iron ore in a hot furnace with carbon. A chemical change will take place. In the end, you get pure iron and carbon dioxide.

People can also use chemical properties to separate elements from solutions. For example, a solution might contain lead, water, and other materials. You might want to remove only the lead. Add another solution that contains iodine. The lead will react with the iodine. They combine to form a compound called lead iodide. It is a yellow solid. You use a filter to remove the lead iodide from the liquid.

Identifying Substances

Scientists can use physical properties such as density to identify materials.

Scientists use chemical properties to identify acids and bases. Acids and bases are two common types of materials. Lemon juice is an acid. Vinegar is an acid. Many house cleaners contain bases. Acids and bases each react with chemicals in special paper. It is called universal indicator paper. Strong acids turn the paper red. Strong bases turn the paper purple. Weaker acids or bases produce different colors.

Universal indicator paper and some other products can tell if a solution is an acid or a base. But it cannot identify a material.

A flame test also gives clues about a material's chemical properties. In a flame test, a substance is heated to high temperatures. Different materials cause the flame to turn different colors. The photograph on page 385 in your textbook demonstrates this with four substances. The color of the flame can help identify each material.

© Pearson Education, Inc. 5

Lesson 3 Checkpoint

1. How can chemical properties be used to separate substances in a mixture or compound?

_____

_____

2. **Draw Conclusions** The chemical reaction for purifying iron ore looks like this:

$$2FeO + C \longrightarrow 2Fe + CO_2$$

   iron   carbon   iron   carbon
   oxide   dioxide

Review the different kinds of reactions discussed in Lesson 2 of your textbook. What kind of reaction is shown here?

_____

_____

3. How might a scientist distinguish the following compounds: strontium chloride and potassium chloride?

_____

_____

4. What color do you think indicator paper would turn if it were dipped in shampoo? Explain your answer.

_____

_____

Lesson 4: How is chemical technology used in our lives?

Vocabulary

polymer a large molecule made of many identical smaller units connected together

Chemistry and Health

Scientists have used chemistry to improve our health. For example, antibiotics are chemicals that can save lives.

Alexander Fleming, a British scientist, discovered antibiotics by accident in 1928. He grew bacteria in dishes. Mold grew in one of his dishes. He noticed that bacteria near the mold died. This mold produced a material that killed bacteria. Chemists found a way to separate this material from the mold. Fleming called the substance penicillin. Penicillin can treat many infections. Today there are many other antibiotics.

Chemists also discovered that vitamins are chemicals in food. People can become ill if they do not get enough vitamins. Because we know more about vitamins these diseases are rare today. Many of our foods have vitamins added.

Fertilizers are chemicals that farmers add to the soil and help food grow. We now have more food to eat because of these chemicals.

Chemistry and New Materials

Scientists use chemistry to create new materials. Silk is a natural material that is soft and strong, but it also burns easily. Nylon is a human-made fabric. It can be used in stockings, fabrics, ropes, nets, and racquet strings.

Nylon is a polymer. A **polymer** is a large molecule. It is made of many smaller units connected together. Plastics are another kind of polymer. Many plastics are made from chemicals in petroleum. Plastics are very useful materials. They are lightweight and last a long time.

Concrete is made with rock sand and water. But it also contains cement, which is a human-made material. Cement makes concrete hard and long-lasting.

Chemistry and Transportation

Scientists use chemistry to improve transportation. We use rubber in tires and shoes. Natural rubber comes from plants. It can bend easily and is waterproof. However, it cracks in cold weather. In the 1800s, chemists learned how to improve rubber. They heated it and added sulfur. In the mid-1900s, chemists started making artificial rubber.

Chemistry helps us use petroleum. Chemists have learned how to break down the larger molecules in petroleum to make gasoline. We use gasoline in cars, buses and motorcycles.

Chemicals and Safety

Many chemicals make our lives better. But chemicals can be dangerous too. Always read warning labels on chemicals, and read directions before you use any cleaner. You might need to wear gloves or goggles. You might need to open a window.

Never mix household cleaners. Mixing cleaners can cause dangerous chemical reactions. These reactions can cause lung damage, burns, and explosions.

Lesson 4 Checkpoint

1. What are antibiotics and how have they improved health?

_____

_____

2. What are three common materials that were developed by scientists?

_____

_____

3. How did scientists working with rubber and petroleum help our modern transportation system?

_____

_____

4. Why is it important to avoid mixing household cleaners?

_____

_____

5. What is a polymer?

_____

_____

6. **Draw Conclusions** Of all the technological developments discussed in this lesson, which one do you think most improved human lives? Explain.

_____

_____

Lesson 1: How can you describe motion?

Vocabulary

velocity the speed and direction of an object's motion

Types of Motion

Motion is movement. When you see something move, you see motion. You move when you walk. You move when you stand up. Your heart moves when it beats. Your eyelids move when you blink. These are all examples of motion.

Motion happens at different rates, or speeds. A sea star moves very slowly. The blades of a fan move very quickly. Some things move so quickly you cannot see them moving.

There are different kinds of motion:

- Constant motion: This motion is steady. The Earth has a constant motion as it moves around the Sun.
- Variable motion: This motion can change direction and speed. A car can move in many different directions. It can also move at many different speeds.
- Periodic motion: This motion moves back and forth. You can tie a weight to a string to make a pendulum. A pendulum swings back and forth.
- Circular motion: Wheels move in a circular motion.
- Vibrational motion: This motion vibrates or moves quickly back and forth in one place. A guitar string vibrates when you play it. A rubber band vibrates when you pluck it.

Speed and Velocity

Average speed is how far an object moves in a given amount of time. Use this formula to calculate average speed:

Average Speed = Distance ÷ Time

For example, a car moved 100 meters in 20 seconds.

Average Speed = 100 meters ÷ 20 seconds

Average Speed = 5 meters per second

Remember, you cannot always see motion. Are you moving when you sit in a chair? Your body is not moving on or off the chair. But you and the chair are on Earth, which is moving quickly around the Sun. So you cannot measure an object's motion only by looking at it. Motion is always measured in relation to some location called a point of reference.

Speed can vary if you change the point of reference. Imagine a person walking on a moving train. If the point of reference is the end of the train, the person is walking at one speed. If the point of reference is a signal light outside the train, the person's speed is much faster.

Velocity describes the speed and direction of an object's motion. The speed of a train might be 30 meters per second. The velocity might be 30 meters per second north. Velocity can also be up or down. A skydiver might have a velocity of 200 kilometers per hour down.

© Pearson Education, Inc. 5

Lesson 1 Checkpoint

1. What are three types of motion?

_____

_____

_____

2. Robert moved 28 meters in 4 seconds. Tallana moved 600 meters in 2 minutes. Javier moved 40 meters in 5 seconds. List these people and their speeds in order from fastest to slowest.

_____

_____

_____

3. What do you need to know to find an object's velocity?

_____

_____

Lesson 2: What are forces?

Vocabulary

force a push or a pull that acts on an object

work the energy used when a force moves an object

power the rate at which work is done

Pushes and Pulls

Forces can move objects. A force can also make an object speed up, slow down, or change direction. A **force** is a push or a pull that acts on an object. Force is measures in newtons (N).

Gravity

Every object has a gravitational pull on every other object. However, only large objects have a gravitational pull you can feel. Earth's gravity pulls objects toward its center. Apples fall down because of Earth's gravity. Gravity also keeps satellites in orbit around Earth.

The Swing of a Pendulum

A pendulum swings because of the force of gravity. When a pendulum starts to swing upward, the force of gravity slows its upward path and pulls it down.

Magnetism and Electricity

Magnetism is a force that pushes and pulls other objects. Every magnet has two poles: a north pole and a south pole. Magnets pull strongly on some materials, such as iron. Magnets also push and pull on other magnets. Opposite poles attract. Matching poles push away from each other.

Electric forces push and pull between objects with electrical charges. Objects will have a negative charge when they gain electrons. If the object loses electrons, it will be positively charged. Electrons often move from one object to another when the objects are rubbed together

An object with a negative charge is attracted to an object with a positive charge.

Gravity, Electricity, and Magnetism

Gravity, magnetism, and electricity can act on an object without touching it. You can block magnetism and electricity with some materials. You cannot block gravity. Magnetism and electricity can push or pull. Gravity has only a pulling force on objects.

Friction

Friction is the force that results when you rub two materials against each other. Friction can slow down motion or keep an object from moving. Air and water resist motion when a moving object pushes against them.

Work and Power

Work is energy used when a force moves an object. Work is equal to the amount of force times the distance the object is forced to move.

Work = Force × Distance

Work is measured in joules. One joule (J) equals the amount of work when 1 newton (N) of force moves an object 1 meter (m).

Power is the rate at which work is done. Power equals the amount of work done divided by the time; the faster the work, the greater the power.

Power = Work ÷ Time

Lesson 2 Checkpoint

1. What are two examples that illustrate Earth's gravitational pull?

_____

_____

2. 🎯 **Cause and Effect** A rock tumbles down a hill. Identify the cause and effect of this event.

_____

_____

3. What are the causes of electric and magnetic forces?

_____

_____

4. 🎯 **Cause and Effect** Describe an event involving electric and magnetic forces. Use your imagination. Describe the cause and effect of each force.

_____

_____

5. How does friction affect movement?

_____

_____

6. What are two examples of forces?

_____

_____

7. What kind of force can make a paper clip cling to a comb?

_____

_____

Lesson 3: What are Newton's laws of motion?

Vocabulary

equilibrium a state in which all the forces on an object balance each other

inertia the tendency of an object to resist any change in motion

acceleration the rate at which the velocity of an object changes over time

Net Forces

More than one force can act on an object at the same time. You roll a ball. Gravity pulls the ball down. Friction slows the ball. Forces can act in different directions. Some forces are stronger than others. The net force is the total of all forces acting on an object. The net force can make an object start moving. The net force determines whether an object will start, stop, or change directions.

Forces can balance each other. One person pushes a box. Another person pushes in the opposite direction. The two forces balance. The box does not move. **Equilibrium** is when the net forces balance. An object that is not moving can be in equilibrium. An object moving at a steady speed in a straight line can also be in equilibrium.

Newton's First Law

Newton's first law of motion describes objects in motion and at rest:

- The First Law of Motion: An object in motion will keep moving unless a net force acts on it. An object at rest will stay at rest until a net force acts on it.

Objects have **inertia.** Heavier objects have more inertia than lighter objects. Inertia keeps things from changing their motion. Think about riding in a car. When you turn a corner, your body is pushed against the side of the car because inertia keeps your body moving in a straight line.

Newton's Second Law

Newton's second law of motion describes how acceleration, mass, and net force are related. **Acceleration** is the rate that velocity changes over time. Net forces can change velocity to speed up, slow down, or change directions. Acceleration measures any of these changes.

- The Second Law of Motion: The net force equals the mass of the object times its acceleration.

Force = mass × acceleration

This law helps us predict how things will move. Imagine pushing a heavy box and a light box. If you use the same force, the light box will move faster. It will have a greater acceleration.

You can also use these related formulas:

acceleration = force ÷ mass
mass = force ÷ acceleration

Newton's Third Law

Newton's third law of motion describes how forces affect each other.

- The Third Law of Motion: When one object exerts a force on a second object, the second object exerts a force on the first object. This law is sometimes called the action-reaction law of motion.

If you lean on a wall, you push on the wall and the wall pushes on you. Forces of you and the wall are equal and opposite.

Lesson 3 Checkpoint

1. How can an object be motionless and in equilibrium?

_____

_____

2. ◎ **Cause and Effect** How can the forces in a game of tug-of-war result in equilibrium?

_____

_____

3. What is inertia? How does it affect the way an object moves?

_____

_____

4. Use Newton's second law of motion to explain what happens when someone pushes a chair across the floor.

_____

_____

5. Which of Newton's laws of motion is demonstrated by a hammer pounding a nail into a board?

_____

_____

6. A satellite orbiting Earth is knocked out of orbit by a meteor. How can Newton's laws of motion be used in describing this event?

_____

_____

_____

7. ◎ **Cause and Effect** What will be the effect of two people pulling on a box with the same amount of force but in opposite directions?

_____

_____

_____

Lesson 4: What are simple machines?

Vocabulary

machine a device that changes the direction or the amount of force needed to do work

Machines and Work

Work is done when a force moves an object. A **machine** can change the direction of the force. It can also change the amount of force needed. Simple machines have only a few parts. Some simple machines include the pulley, wheel and axle, inclined plane, and lever.

Machines do not make the amount of work less. However, they can make it easier to do the work.

Pulley

A pulley is a simple machine. It has a rope or cable and a wheel. The wheel has a groove. The rope fits into the groove. A pulley makes work easier by changing the direction of the force. When you pull down on the rope, the object moves up.

Wheel and Axle

A wheel and axle is another simple machine. The wheel has a circular shape. The axle is a straight bar. A wheel and axle reduces the amount of force needed to do work. A doorknob is a wheel and axle. A well uses a wheel and axle to lift a bucket of water. The steering wheel of a car is also a wheel and axle.

Lever

A lever is another type of simple machine. A lever has a stiff bar that moves around a fixed point. This point is called the fulcrum. A see-saw is a lever. You can put a box on one side. If you push down on the other side, the box moves up. As the position of the fulcrum changes, the amount of force needed will change. If you move the fulcrum closer to the box, the lever will be easier to use.

A lever makes it easier to do work. If you use a lever, you use less force.

Inclined Planes

An inclined plane is another simple machine. It has a flat surface, with one end higher than the other. A ramp is an inclined plane. It is easier to push a box up an inclined plane than to lift it. A doorstop is also an inclined plane. A screw uses an inclined plane. A tiny incline plane wraps around the screw.

Complex Machines

A complex machine uses two or more simple machines. Complex machines can use many forces to do work, such as electricity, gravity, human force, or magnetism. They may also burn fuel.

A go cart is a complex machine that includes many simple machines. The steering wheel is a wheel and axle. The pedals are levers. The cart burns fuel to do work.

A sailboat is another complex machine. The parts of a sailboat work together. Pulleys lift the sails. The rudder is a lever that steers the ship. A wheel and axle move the rudder.

© Pearson Education, Inc. 5

Lesson 4 Checkpoint

1. What are two examples of a wheel and axle that can make work easier?

   _____

   _____

2. What are the parts of a lever?

   _____

   _____

3. Why is a screw considered a simple machine?

   _____

   _____

4. Name one complex machine and two of the simple machines that make it up.

   _____

   _____

   _____

5. **⦿ Cause and Effect** When you use a screwdriver to open the lid of a paint can, the *cause* is the force you apply to the screwdriver and the *effect* is the lid coming off. Describe the cause and effect of using some other simple machine.

   _____

   _____

   _____

Name _____

Lesson 1: What is energy?

Vocabulary

energy ability to do work or cause a change, it cannot be created or destroyed

kinetic energy energy due to motion

potential energy energy that could cause change in the future

Forms of Energy

Energy is the ability to do work or cause a change. Energy can change an object's motion, color, shape, temperature, or other qualities.

There are many forms of energy. Chemical energy is found in the bonds that hold molecules together. Nuclear energy holds the nucleus of an atom together. Mechanical energy is in moving or stretching objects.

Energy can change forms. Some of this energy is given off as heat. For example, a lamp changes electrical energy to light energy. Some of this light energy changes to thermal energy, or heat. You can measure this change by feeling the light bulb. An object that gains thermal energy becomes warmer.

Kinetic Energy

Kinetic energy, the energy of moving things, is greater when an object moves faster. An object with more mass has more kinetic energy.

Kinetic energy can change into other kinds of energy. A windmill changes kinetic energy into electric energy. Rubbing your hands causes kinetic energy to change into thermal energy. Your hands get warmer.

Potential Energy

Potential energy is stored energy. It is not causing any changes now, but can cause changes later. There are many kinds of potential energy.

Gravitational energy is one kind of potential energy. A metal ball hanging from a string is not causing changes now. But it will cause changes to the clay underneath when it falls. An object has more gravitational potential energy when it is higher off the ground.

Potential energy does not disappear when an object falls. It changes into other forms of energy. A toy car at the top of a track is not moving. It has potential energy that changes into kinetic energy when the car falls down the track. Some of this kinetic energy changes into sound energy and thermal energy.

Chemical Energy

Potential energy can be in the form of chemical energy. Remember that bonds form when atoms share electrons. Bonds can also form when electrons move from one atom to another. A bond that has more electrons will have more chemical energy.

Fuels have chemical energy. Some fuels have more energy than others. Food is fuel for your body. Some foods give your body more energy than others.

Nuclear Energy

The nucleus of an atom contains huge amounts of potential energy. An atom's nucleus contains protons and neutrons. When a proton is knocked out of its nucleus, nuclear energy is released.

© Pearson Education, Inc. 5

Lesson 1 Checkpoint

1. What are some different kinds of energy?

_____

_____

2. 🎯 **Predict** What does the energy of a light bulb change into after the lamp has been lit for a while? How can you measure the change?

_____

_____

3. Why do your hands get warmer when you rub them together?

_____

_____

4. What are some types of potential energy?

_____

_____

5. How does chemical energy hold molecules together?

_____

_____

6. How does the energy in an apple compare to the energy in the other foods listed on page 453 in your textbook?

_____

_____

Lesson 2: What is sound energy?

What Is Sound?

Sound is a wave of vibrations that spread from their source. A vibration is a back-and-forth movement.

Sound waves are made of particles. The particles in a sound wave move in a pattern. They get closer together and then move farther apart. The areas where particles are close together are called crests. The number of crests that pass a point in one second is the frequency. Pitch is how high or low a sound is. A sound's pitch is higher when the sound has a greater frequency.

Why are some sounds louder than others? The source of the louder sounds is vibrating more. These sound waves have more energy. The energy squeezes the particles at the crests closer together.

Your Voice

As air rushes past your vocal cords, your vocal cords vibrate. Your vocal cords make the particles in the air around them vibrate. These vibrations travel through the air as sound waves. Sound waves travel in all directions. People in front of you can hear you speak. People behind you can hear this sound too.

How Does Sound Behave?

Sound can move through water and metal, and many other materials. But sound cannot move through vacuum. A vacuum is empty space without particles. Sound cannot be made without particles.

When sound waves reach a border between different materials, they can bounce back from the border, they can be absorbed, or the sound can pass into the second material.

Sound waves can bounce back when they hit a surface, such as a wall. This reflection may cause an echo.

Sound can also be absorbed, or soaked up by a material. For example, you may not hear footsteps when you walk on a carpet. The carpet absorbs the sound.

Moving from one material to another material changes the speed of a sound wave. The sound wave's speed depends on what the materials are made of. For example, sound moves more slowly in air than in water, depending on the temperature.

Sound Transfers Energy

Sound waves transfer energy from one object to another. For example, the kinetic energy of piano keys make the piano's strings vibrate. This creates sound energy. Special walls in a music room are lined with soundproofing materials. The piano's sound bounces off the material many times. The material vibrates each time it bounces, creating thermal energy. The material absorbs almost all of the sound waves that hit it. This causes the sound to lessen.

Sound begins with a vibrating object. The object gives off energy in sound waves in air. As the sound waves move, the energy is transferred through the air. Some of the energy reaches your ear. Your eardrum absorbs some of the energy. Your eardrum begins to vibrate, and you receive the energy of the original vibrating object.

Lesson 2 Checkpoint

1. Describe a sound you have heard. State its cause and describe its frequency and loudness.

_____

_____

_____

2. What happens when sound waves hit a wall?

_____

_____

_____

3. Describe a time you observed the transmission, reflection, or absorption of a sound.

_____

_____

_____

4. 🎯 **Predict** When sound waves travel from air to water what will happen to the speed at which they are moving?

_____

_____

_____

Lesson 3: What is light energy?

Vocabulary

electromagnetic radiation a combination of electrical and magnetic energy

Electromagnetic Radiation

Light is like sound in some ways. Light moves in waves. Light waves have wavelengths and frequencies. The speed of light changes when it moves through different materials. Light can be reflected or absorbed by certain objects. Or, light can pass through them.

Unlike sound, light is not a vibration of particles. Light is a form of **electromagnetic radiation.** This means light energy is made of electrical and magnetic energy.

The electromagnetic spectrum is a range of waves that have many frequencies and wavelengths. Visible light makes up a small part of the electromagnetic spectrum. Visible light is light that you can see. Different wavelengths of visible light are seen as different colors.

Ultraviolet, X ray, and gamma ray radiation have shorter wavelengths than wavelengths of visible light. Shorter wavelengths have higher frequencies and more energy than visible light.

Infrared waves, microwaves, and radio waves have longer wavelengths than wavelengths of visible light. Longer waves have lower frequencies and lower energies than visible light.

How Does Light Move?

Like sound, the speed of light changes when it moves through different materials. Unlike sound, light can travel through a vacuum. The speed of light is fastest in a vacuum. Light travels more slowly through materials such as air or water.

Three things can happen when light hits an object. The light can reflect, refract, or be absorbed.

Light moves in a straight line, even when it reflects off an object, such as a mirror. But the light moves in a different direction.

Light bends when it enters a new material. This is called refraction. A prism is a clear object that refracts light. It separates light into different wavelengths. A prism changes white lights into different colors. It makes a rainbow.

A lens is another clear object that bends light. A concave lens is thickest in the middle. A concave lens bends light. It makes objects look larger. A convex lens is thinner in the middle. It bends light to make objects look smaller.

A shadow is an object in the path of light. Light waves bend at the edges of the object. This causes the shadow to fall behind the object. A shadow gets bigger if the object moves closer to the light.

Some materials absorb light. This changes the light energy into thermal energy. Some light frequencies are not absorbed. They can pass through the material or are reflected off the material. This creates the colors we see. For example, a red shirt absorbs many light frequencies. But it reflects red light.

© Pearson Education, Inc. **5**

Lesson 3 Checkpoint

1. How is light energy like sound energy?

_____

_____

_____

2. What happens to light as it passes through a prism?

_____

_____

_____

3. How does light move?

_____

_____

4. ⊙ **Predict** How would a shadow change as an object moved toward the light source?

_____

_____

_____

Lesson 4: What is thermal energy?

Vocabulary

thermal energy the total of all the kinetic and potential energy of the atoms in an object

conduction the transfer of heat between objects that are in contact

convection the transfer of heat by a moving liquid or gas

When Matter Gets Warmer

Kinetic energy is the energy of motion. The atoms in a potato have kinetic energy. These atoms are always moving. They move faster if you heat the potato. This means the kinetic energy of the atoms increases. The thermal energy of the atoms also increases. **Thermal energy** is all the kinetic and potential energy in an object's atoms.

A warmer object has more thermal energy than a cooler object. For example, water vapor is warmer than ice. This means that the atoms in the water vapor are moving faster that the atoms in the ice.

Thermal Energy and Phase Changes

Matter can be solid, liquid, or a gas. Matter can change to a different phase when its thermal energy changes.

An object's particles move faster when its thermal energy increases. If a solid melts into a liquid its thermal energy increases.

The liquid's particles will move faster if the liquid gets warmer. The liquid will change into a gas if its thermal energy increases enough.

Thermal Energy and Temperature

Temperature is a measure of thermal energy. The temperature of an object tells you about the kinetic energy of its particles.

People use thermometers to measure temperature. Many thermometers are closed tubes. They contain a liquid, such as mercury or alcohol. The liquid expands at higher temperatures. The height of the liquid inside the tube shows the temperature.

Conduction, Convection, Radiation

Thermal energy naturally moves from warmer substances to cooler ones. People use the word *heat* to talk about thermal energy. Heat can move by conduction, convection, and radiation.

- Conduction is the flow of heat between objects that are touching. For example, you might put a cold metal spoon in a hot pan. The pan's particles are moving faster than the spoon's particles. The warmer particles give some of their thermal energy to the spoon. This makes the temperature of the pan decrease. But, the temperature of the spoon increases. Heat will keep moving until the objects have the same temperature.

- Convection is another way that heat moves. Convection is the movement of warm liquids or gases to cooler areas. For example, suppose you have a fish tank. The heater warms the water next to it by conduction. This warm water carries heat to the rest of the tank's water by convection.

- Radiation is the movement of energy by electromagnetic waves.

© Pearson Education, Inc. 5

Quick Study

Name _____

Lesson 4 Checkpoint

1. What is the relationship between the temperature of an object and the motion of its particles?

_____

_____

_____

2. Which most likely has greater thermal energy, ice or water vapor? Why?

_____

_____

_____

3. What examples of conduction, convection, or radiation can you find in your classroom?

_____

_____

_____

Lesson 1: What are the effects of moving charges?

Vocabulary

current the flow of electrical charges through a material

conductor a material through which an electric charge can move easily

resistor a material that resists the flow of an electric charge

insulator strong resistor that can stop most electrical currents

Electric Charges

Atoms have protons and electrons. Protons have a positive charge. Electrons have a negative charge. Most atoms have the same number of protons and electrons. This means the atom is neutral. But atoms often lose and gain electrons. This causes an atom to have a positive or negative charge. When an atom loses an electron, it has more protons than electrons. This means the atom has a positive charge. If the atom gains an electron, it has more electrons than protons and now has a negative charge.

What happens when you rub a balloon on your hair? Electrons break away from your hair. Now your hair has a positive charge. The negative electrons move to the balloon. The balloon now has a negative charge. Opposite charges attract. The balloon sticks to your hair.

Rub two balloons on your hair. Hold them together. You will feel a small force pushing the balloons apart because the balloons have the same, negative charge.

The flow of charges between your hair and the balloon is an example of static electricity. Moving charges are usually used in electrical currents. These currents run through wires. **Current** is the flow of electrical charges through a material

Electric charges can move easily through a **conductor.** Conductors have some electrons that are not tightly joined to their atoms. These electrons move inside the conductor easily. This causes electrons to join themselves to other atoms. These atoms now have different charges.

Metals such as copper, gold, silver, and aluminum are some of the best conductors. Electric wires are often made of copper and aluminum. Pure metals are often better conductors than mixed metals.

Pencil lead can also conduct electrical current. Some liquids and gases are conductors too. Salt water can conduct electrical current.

Some metals are not good conductors. A material that fights the flow of an electric charge is called a **resistor.** A resistor can make electrical energy change to thermal energy. Toasters heat bread because of resistors. A toaster has wires made of nickel and chrome that fight electrical current. This changes the electrical energy into thermal energy and heats the bread.

An **insulator** is a strong resistor and can stop most electrical currents. Some insulators are rubber, plastic, glass, and dry cotton. Rubber insulation is often wrapped around wires that carry electrical energy. This makes it safe for people to use these wires.

All materials usually have some resistance to electrical energy. Even good conductors can have some resistance. A superconductor is a material that has no resistance to electrical current. We can change metals into superconductors by cooling them. The materials lose their resistance at very low temperatures.

© Pearson Education, Inc. 5

Lesson 1 Checkpoint

1. What causes an atom to have a negative or positive charge?

_____

_____

_____

2. What is an electrical current?

_____

_____

_____

3. Name three materials that are used as conductors and three that are used as insulators.

_____

_____

_____

4. **Cause and Effect** What effect might be caused by electrons being loosely bound to atoms in a material?

_____

_____

_____

Lesson 2: What are simple circuits?

Vocabulary

circuit diagram a map of a circuit, it shows parts and path of an electric circuit

volt a measure of the electrical energy provided by an energy source

Parts of a Circuit

A circuit moves electrical energy from one place to another in a looped path. A simple circuit always has a source of energy and a conductor.

A battery can provide the energy to move electric charges through a circuit. A battery has chemicals that can make a current. The current leaves the negative end of the battery and moves to the positive end of the battery.

A circuit can have more than one conductor. A conductor makes an unbroken path in the circuit. Charges will not flow in a broken circuit.

A circuit can also have a switch that opens or closes a gap in the circuit. Closing the gap lets the electric charges flow. Opening the gap stops the current.

Most circuits also have resistors. A resistor transforms energy to electrical energy into sound, light, thermal, or mechanical energy. A light bulb is a resistor. It changes electrical energy into light energy. A buzzer is another resistor. It changes electrical energy into sound energy.

Circuit Diagrams

A **circuit diagram** is a map of a circuit. People use circuit diagrams to help build circuits. The lines on a circuit diagram show how electricity moves through the circuit. The symbols on a circuit diagram show different parts of the circuit. The chart on page 484 in your textbook shows some of these symbols. For example, the symbol for a wire looks like a line. The symbol for a resistor is an uneven line.

The **volt** is a measure of the electrical energy a source makes. Many batteries make about 1.5 volts of electricity. Small, square batteries make about 9 volts of electricity.

Ohms measure the amount of resistance to an electrical current. A flashlight bulb has about 20 ohms of resistance.

The current in the circuit is measured in amperes, also called amps. Current is measured by how much charge moves past a certain spot each second.

Series Circuits

A circuit can have more than one resistor. A circuit with more than one resistor is called a series circuit.

Lesson 2 Checkpoint

1. If the switch is left open, what happens to the current?

_____

_____

2. Name four common parts of an electric circuit.

_____

_____

_____

_____

3. Describe the purpose of a resistor in a circuit.

_____

_____

_____

Lesson 3: What are complex circuits?

Vocabulary

electromagnet magnets made by an electrical current

Parallel Circuits

A parallel circuit is complex and has more than one path. Some parallel circuits have hundreds of paths. For example, computers have very complex paths. A computer chip is the size of a stamp. But it can hold millions of paths and resistors.

Every branch of a parallel circuit can hold one or more resistors. Parallel circuits have more resistors than a series circuit.

All the paths of a parallel circuit do not have to be on at the same time. Switches can control different parts of the circuit. Some paths can be turned on when others are turned off.

Electrical Safety: Avoid These Shocking Hazards

- Do not touch electrical outlets. Cover unused outlets with safety caps.
- Always pull the plug out of an outlet. Do not pull on the cord. It may damage the wires.
- Immediately replace old cords.
- Never touch a power line.
- Never touch an electrical machine if you are standing in water.
- Do not use electrical appliances near water.

Electromagnets

Every electrical current produces a magnetic force. Electrical current makes electromagnets. **Electromagnets** are made when a current flows through a coiled wire in a circuit. This changes the electrical energy into magnetic energy.

One way to make an electromagent is to use a wire with more coils or to increase the current. Another way to make an electromagnet stronger is by adding a metal bar inside the coils.

An electromagnet is different from a regular magnet. You cannot turn a regular magnet on and off. But you can turn an electromagnet on and off. Unlike a regular magnet, you can change the strength of an electromagnet. Like all magnets, an electromagnet has a north and a south pole.

Ways We Use Electromagnets

We use electromagnets in many ways. We use electromagnets in motors, sound systems, and even doorbells. The electromagnets in a motor turn on and off quickly. This causes parts of the motor to spin. The electrical energy turns into mechanical energy. Motors can move many things. They can move toy cars as well as huge trains.

Lesson 3 Checkpoint

1. Describe a parallel circuit.

_____

_____

2. How is a parallel circuit different from a series circuit?

_____

_____

3. What are two ways to make an electromagnet stronger?

_____

_____

4. 🎯 **Cause and Effect** What is the effect of an electromagnet in a motor?

_____

_____

Lesson 1: What is the history of astronomy?

Patterns In the Sky

There are patterns in the sky. Patterns are repeated events. The Sun rises and sets each day. The Moon has phases. The seasons change. Long ago, people made calendars based on these cycles.

Eclipses

A solar eclipse takes place when the Moon blocks the Sun's light. A lunar eclipse occurs when Earth's shadow falls on the Moon. Long ago, people thought these rare eclipses were signs predicting trouble.

Astronomy Around the World

Ancient people did not write about what they saw in the sky. But their buildings show us how important the movements in the sky were to them.

Stonehenge is a giant circle of stones in England. People began building it about 35,000 years ago. Stonehenge shows that ancient peoples knew the cycles of the Sun and the seasons. For example, some of the stones point to where the Sun rises on the longest day of the year.

About 700 years ago, people built a pyramid in Chichén Itzá, in a place that is now Mexico. This pyramid shows that people watched the sky and knew the times of year when the number of daylight and nighttime hours were equal.

Early Tools

People invented tools to help them study the stars. The astrolabe was a tool that helped scientists predict where stars would be on a certain day or when the Sun would rise or set. Later, scientists used a sextant to study the sky.

Galileo Galilei was the first person to use a telescope in astronomy. A telescope makes objects in the sky look larger. Galileo learned that Jupiter had four moons, and that Venus had phases like the Moon. This meant that Earth and the planets move around the Sun. Most people thought the Sun and planets move around Earth.

Isaac Newton, another scientist, invented the reflecting telescope. It had a curved mirror that helped people see objects dimmer and farther away.

Today's High-Tech Telescopes

Telescopes work because they collect light. The light we see from the Sun or stars is called visible light. But it is only a fraction of the light in the universe. Most objects in space make light that we cannot see, called electromagnetic radiation. Radio waves and infrared radiation are two kinds of electromagnetic radiation. Special new telescopes can see this light.

Keck I and Keck II are the world's largest telescopes. Each telescope has a huge mirror to gather light. This mirror is made of 36 pieces that work together. Both telescopes are used to study faraway stars.

Radio telescopes do not have a mirror or lens. They use dishes to collect radio waves. They often have many dishes that work together.

Earth's atmosphere contains dust and other materials that block light. Telescopes on Earth must look through this dust. Scientists launch telescopes into space to get clearer pictures.

© Pearson Education, Inc. 5

Lesson 1 Checkpoint

1. What is a solar eclipse? a lunar eclipse?

    _____

    _____

2. What did ancient peoples leave behind that tells us that the cycles of the Sun, Moon, and stars were important to them?

    _____

    _____

3. ⊙ **Summarize** what you have learned about the astronomical observations of ancient cultures.

    _____

    _____

4. What did Galileo conclude from his observations of Jupiter and Venus?

    _____

    _____

5. How are radio telescopes different from the Keck telescopes?

    _____

    _____

6. Why must certain types of telescopes be sent into space?

    _____

    _____

Lesson 2: What is a star?

Vocabulary

light-year the distance light travels in one year

nebula a cloud of gas and dust from which new stars form

supernova a gigantic explosion that occurs after a large star's core runs out of fuel

black hole a point in space with such a strong force of gravity that nothing within a certain distance can escape getting sucked into it

How the Sun Stacks Up as a Star

The Sun is a star. All stars are very large balls of hot gases that give off electromagnetic radiation. The Sun gives off huge amounts of heat and light energy. Very high heat and pressure push hydrogen atoms together, creating helium. Huge amounts of energy are let go as this happens, making the Sun shine.

Brightness, Color, and Temperature of Stars

The Sun is the closest star to Earth and the brightest. The brightest stars give off the most energy. How bright a star looks depends on the star's size, temperature, and distance from Earth. For example, Sirius is larger, hotter, and brighter than the Sun. But it is the ninth closest star to Earth.

Red stars are the coolest. Orange and yellow stars are hotter. The hottest stars are white or blue-white, like Sirius. Sirius does not look brighter than the Sun because it is much farther from us than the Sun.

Distance is measured in **light-years** which is the distance light travels in one year, which is over 9 trillion kilometers.

The Explosive Sun

The Sun's innermost layer is called the photosphere. It gives off the light we see. The layer above the photosphere is the chromosphere. The outer layer is called the corona.

Sunspots are dark spots that are part of the photosphere and are cooler than the rest of the photosphere. Sunspots travel across the Sun indicating that the Sun rotates slower at its poles than it does at its equator.

Solar Eruptions

Ribbons of gas called prominence leap out of the chromosphere. The chromosphere can also erupt like a volcano. This is a solar flare. It can last for minutes or hours.

The Life of Stars

New stars form in a nebula. A **nebula** is a cloud of dust and gas pulled together by gravity. The temperature rises. Hydrogen changes into helium. The particles release energy. The particles become a star.

A star can use up all of its hydrogen and helium and die. The center of the star may shrink and cool. It becomes a white dwarf star. The star will take millions of years to become cold. Then it becomes a black dwarf star.

A very large star can run out of helium. Then it shrinks in on itself. Suddenly, the star stops shrinking. This causes a great explosion called a **supernova.** A star can also die when the core of a large star shrinks in on itself until it becomes a black hole. Nothing can escape getting sucked into a **black hole**—not even light.

© Pearson Education, Inc. **5**

Lesson 2 Checkpoint

1. Which star is hotter, a yellow star or a white star?

   _____

2. What does the way sunspots travel across the face of the Sun indicate about the way the Sun rotates?

   _____

   _____

3. What is the Sun?

   _____

   _____

4. Where does a new star form?

   _____

   _____

5. ⦿ **Summarize** the three ways a star might die.

   _____

   _____

   _____

Use with pp. 524–529

Lesson 3: How are stars grouped together?
Vocabulary

galaxy a huge system of stars, dust, and gas held together by gravity

constellation an area of the sky and all the stars seen in that area

Galaxies

A **galaxy** is a huge group of stars, dust, and gases. Gravity holds a galaxy together. There are billions of galaxies. Earth is part of the Milky Way galaxy.

About three-fourths of the galaxies are spiral galaxies with wide centers. They also have thin arms that stretch out from the center like a pinwheel. Stars are in these arms. The stars move around the center of the galaxy. The Milky Way is a spiral galaxy.

Elliptical galaxies are round or oval. They can look like footballs. The largest galaxies are elliptical. There are also elliptical galaxies that are smaller than the Milky Way.

Some galaxies are called irregular because they are not spiral or elliptical. They do not have a definite shape. Irregular galaxies are probably young galaxies with their stars are still forming.

Constellations

Ursa Major is part of the Milky Way galaxy. Ursa Major is a constellation. A **constellation** is an area of the sky and all the stars seen in that area. A constellation is like a star's address. Scientists use constellations to help them locate stars. For example, the Big Dipper is part of the constellation Ursa Major. There are 88 constellations.

From Earth, the stars in a constellation may look close together. They may look this way because they are in the same direction from Earth. But the stars might actually be very far apart.

People in different parts of the world see different constellations. Earth can be divided into two parts along the equator. The half to the north of the equator is called the Northern Hemisphere. The half to the south of the equator is called the Southern Hemisphere. The United States is in the Northern Hemisphere. Ursa Major can be seen in the Northern Hemisphere. But people in the Southern Hemisphere cannot see it. The constellation Centaurus can be seen only in the Southern Hemisphere.

Stars on the Move

You can see Ursa Major all year. But other constellations can only be seen at certain times of the year. Canis Major is a constellation we see only in the winter.

The constellations change with the seasons. This is because Earth rotates, or spins. It takes Earth one year to move around the Sun. We see different parts of the sky as Earth moves.

Nothing in the universe stands still. Stars hurtle though space at different speeds and in different directions. We cannot see this movement because the stars are too far away. Over time, the patterns of the stars will change. Some stars will move closer together or farther apart.

© Pearson Education, Inc. 5

Lesson 3 Checkpoint

1. What type of galaxy is the Milky Way?

   _____

2. Which constellation is the Big Dipper in?

   _____

3. Which type of galaxy is almost round or football shaped?

   _____

4. How many constellations are there?

   _____

5. Compare and Contrast Ursa Major and the Milky Way.

   _____

   _____

   _____

Lesson 1: In what ways does Earth move?

Vocabulary

solar system the Sun and its nine planets along with many moons, asteroids, and comets

revolution one full orbit around the Sun

axis an imaginary center line

rotation one whole spin of an object on its axis

Earth's Orbit

Earth is one of nine planets that move around the Sun. The Sun, planets, moons, asteroids, and comets make up the **solar system.**

Each planet moves in a path around the Sun. This is called an orbit. Gravity keeps the planets in their orbits. The shape of each orbit is elliptical, like a flattened circle.

One complete orbit around the Sun is called a **revolution.** Earth's revolution around the Sun takes about 365 days, one year. The Moon revolves around Earth. The Moon's revolution takes about 28 days, which is about a month.

Day and Night

Earth, like all planets, spins. This causes part of Earth to face the Sun. This is day. Soon, that same part of Earth faces away from the Sun. This is night.

Earth spins on an axis. An **axis** is an imaginary center line. One complete spin on its axis is called a **rotation**. Earth takes about 24 hours, or one day, to complete one rotation.

Earth's Comfortable Temperature

Earth rotates quickly, so day and night follow each other fairly fast. This helps keep the temperature we need in order to live. Earth would have hotter days and colder nights if it rotated more slowly. Other planets get very hot or very cold.

Earth is also unlike other planets in that it has an atmosphere. It reflects some of the Sun's rays. This keeps Earth from getting too hot. The atmosphere also traps some of the Sun's rays. This keeps Earth from getting too cold.

The Pattern of Seasons

What causes the seasons? Earth always tilts the same way as it orbits the Sun. The tilt causes different parts of Earth to face the Sun during different seasons. This means the number of daylight hours change during the year. There are more daylight hours in summer and fewer daylight hours in winter.

Earth's tilt also causes light from the Sun to hit parts of Earth at different angles. The amount of sunlight an area receives creates its climate. The equator receives the most direct sunlight. The Sun's rays are more spread out when they hit the poles. This causes the poles to have a colder climate than the equator.

Earth's Seasons

There are four seasons in the Northern Hemisphere: spring, summer, fall, and winter.

The North Pole is closest to the Sun on the first day of summer. The South Pole is closest to the Sun on the first day of winter.

© Pearson Education, Inc. 5

Lesson 1 Checkpoint

1. What is the shape of the planets' orbits?

   _____

2. What causes day and night?

   _____

   _____

3. What is the season in the Northern Hemisphere when the North Pole points most directly toward the Sun?

   _____

4. How is the climate near the equator different from the climate near the poles? What causes this difference?

   _____

   _____

Lesson 2: What are the parts of the solar system?

Vocabulary

space probe spacecraft that gather data without a crew

The Solar System

All nine planets are part of the solar system. They all orbit the Sun. The inner planets are closer to the Sun. Their orbits are smaller. These planets can complete a revolution quickly. The inner planets are:

- Mercury: This planet is closest to the Sun. Mercury is a small, rocky planet with many craters.
- Venus: Hot clouds cover the surface of this rocky planet.
- Earth: Earth is solid and rocky. Water and ice cover 75% of its surface. A thin layer of air surrounds Earth.
- Mars: This planet is rocky. Red soil covers this planet, sometimes called the "Red Planet."

Outer planets are farther from the Sun. They move more slowly than the inner planets. Their orbits take longer. This means their years last longer. The outer planets are:

- Jupiter: Jupiter is the largest "gas giant." It is called a gas giant because it is mostly made of hydrogen, helium, and other gases.
- Saturn: Saturn like all gas giants, has rings of rock, dust, and ice. Saturn has the most rings.
- Uranus: Methane gas gives this gas giant its blue-green color.

- Neptune: Neptune is also a gas giant. It gives off more energy than it gets from the Sun.
- Pluto: Pluto is a small, rocky planet about the size of Earth's moon. Pluto, farthest from the Sun, is the smallest and coldest planet in the Solar system.

Visiting the Planets

Scientists use space probes to explore the planets. A **space probe** is a spacecraft that has instruments and cameras to collect information about the planets. This is some of the information we have learned from space probes:

- Mercury has almost no atmosphere. Its temperature can be as cold as –170°C or as hot as 970°C.
- Venus has a thick, cloudy atmosphere made of poisonous gases. The clouds trap the Sun's heat. So the planet's temperature is the same day and night.
- Mars has a very thin atmosphere made mostly of carbon dioxide. It also has very large volcanoes and polar ice caps.
- Jupiter, Saturn, Uranus, and Neptune are the four gas giants. These gas planets have many moons and rings.
- Pluto is made of rock and ice. Its moon is almost the same size as it is, which is why it is sometimes called a "double planet."

Lesson 2 Checkpoint

1. List the order of the planets from nearest to farthest from the Sun. Look at pages 549–550 in your textbook for help.

_____

_____

2. 🎯 **Make Inferences** Why do the planets have years of different lengths?

_____

_____

3. Name the planets that have solid surfaces and give another detail about each.

_____

_____

_____

4. Compare and contrast the inner planets with the outer planets, excluding Pluto. List at least two ways they are similar, and at least two differences.

_____

_____

_____

Lesson 3: What are comets and asteroids?

Vocabulary

comet a frozen mass of different types of ice and dust orbiting the Sun

asteroid a rocky mass up to several hundred kilometers wide that revolves around the Sun

Comets

A **comet** is a frozen mass of ice and dust. Comets orbit the Sun. They are much smaller than planets. Comets come from areas beyond Pluto. Every year, several comets travel into the solar system. Comets move in very long, oval paths. Only a few are large enough to be seen without a telescope.

How are comets discovered? People use telescopes to take pictures of the sky. They are able to see comets in these pictures.

A comet has three main parts:

- Nucleus: This is the center of a comet. It is very small. It is made of dust and ice.
- Coma: The coma is a huge cloud of dust and evaporated gases that surrounds the nucleus. It forms when the comet gets close to the Sun. The Sun melts the nucleus. The coma makes the comet look bright and fuzzy.
- Tails: A comet has two long tails. The ion tail is made of gases. It glows. Ion tails are thin and blue. The dust tail is made of dust that comes from the nucleus as it melts. A dust tail is wide and yellow.

The tails are pushed out by solar wind, which is made of moving particles from the Sun. A comet's tails can become 80 million kilometers long. The tails may become shorter as the comet moves farther away from the Sun.

Asteroids

Unlike a comet, an **asteroid** is a rocky mass that orbits the Sun. Asteroids are smaller than planets. Sometimes, they are called minor planets. Unlike comets, most asteroids orbit in the asteroid belt. This is an area between Mars and Jupiter.

Can asteroids hit Earth? Yes. Asteroids can form huge craters when they hit Earth. However, this is very rare. Jupiter's gravity holds most asteroids in the asteroid belt.

Meteors, Meteoroids, and Meteorites

A meteoroid is a small asteroid. A meteoroid can be the size of a very large rock but most are the size of pebbles or grains of sand. Have you ever seen a shooting star? Shooting stars are not really stars. They are meteors. A meteor forms when a meteoroid hits the Earth's atmosphere. The meteoroid heats up quickly. It gets so hot that it glows as a streak of light. Very bright meteors are called fireballs.

Meteor showers happen at certain times each year. This happens when Earth passes through the orbit of a comet. A comet loses dust and rocky matter when it heats up. These loose pieces stay in the comet's orbit. They become meteors when they hit Earth's atmosphere.

Most meteors burn up before they hit Earth's surface. Some meteors do not burn up completely. They may fall to Earth. A meteorite is a piece of a meteor that lands on Earth. Most meteorites are small. The largest known meteorite fell in Africa. It weighed 60 tons.

© Pearson Education, Inc. **5**

Lesson 3 Checkpoint

1. Describe a comet's orbit and the changes that occur to a comet during an orbit.

_____

_____

_____

_____

2. ◎ **Make Inferences** about how the size of a comet's tail changes during its orbit.

_____

_____

3. Describe two differences between comets and asteroids.

_____

_____

4. Explain at least two ways that comets and asteroids can affect Earth.

_____

_____

_____

Lesson 4: What is known about the Moon?

Vocabulary

satellite a moon, rock, or anything that orbits another object

Moon phases the shapes of the lit side of the Moon we can see

Traveling with Earth

The Moon is smaller than Earth. It is about one-fourth of Earth's size. Unlike Earth, the Moon has no air or water. The moon is a satellite. A **satellite** orbits another object. A satellite can be a moon, a rock, or any object. The Moon is Earth's only natural satellite. Earth's other satellites are man-made.

The Moon's Surface

The surface of the Moon is rocky. There are craters, valleys, mountains, and plains. Rocks or comets that hit the Moon made these craters. Unlike Earth's craters, the Moon's craters last millions of years because there is no air or water to wear them away.

Looking at the Moon

We only see one side of the Moon. The "near side" always faces Earth because the Moon's spin and orbit happen at the same speed. It takes about 29 days for the Moon to revolve around Earth. It also takes 29 days for the Moon to spin once on its axis.

Astronauts have seen the "far side" of the moon. In 1969, U.S. astronaut Neil Armstrong was the first human to walk on the Moon. So far, 12 people have walked on the Moon.

Phases of the Moon

The Moon does not make its own light. It reflects the Sun's light. **Moon phases** are the shapes of the lit side of the Moon we can see. The phases of the Moon are predictable as they repeat about every 29 days. The position of Earth, the Moon, and the Sun create these phases.

- New Moon: The Moon is passing between Earth and the Sun. Its sunlit side is facing away from Earth.
- Crescent Moon: A small piece of the Moon's sunlit side faces Earth.
- First Quarter: Half of the Moon's sunlit side faces Earth. This happens about a week after the New Moon.
- Full Moon: Earth is between the Moon and the Sun. The Moon's entire lighted side faces Earth. This happens about two weeks after the New Moon.

High and Low Tides

Most places on Earth have two high tides and two low tides each day. The Moon's gravity causes these tides. Earth's land, water, and air are pulled toward the Moon.

The difference between high tide and low tide in the ocean is about two feet. Along the coast, the shape of the land affects the tides. In many places, high tide is about two meters (six feet) higher than low tide. In some places, the difference is much greater.

The Sun's gravity also affects tides. However, the Sun is very far away. Its effect is much smaller than the Moon's effect.

Tides also change with the Moon's phases. Tides are highest during a full Moon or a new Moon. At these times, the Sun, Earth, and the Moon line up. The gravity of both the Moon and the Sun pull in the same direction.

Lesson 4 Checkpoint

1. Why do we not see the "far side" of the Moon?

_____

_____

2. Are the Moon phases predictable? Why or why not?

_____

_____

3. 🎯 **Infer** how the appearance of Earth would change if you watched it from the near side of the Moon for a month.

_____

_____

4. Which phases of the Moon bring the highest tides? What causes the high tides?

_____

_____

5. Describe 3 ways the Moon is different from Earth.

_____

_____

Lesson 1: What is technology?

Vocabulary

technology the use of scientific knowledge for a purpose

inventor someone who uses technology to develop a new device or process, or to solve a problem

manufacturing the production of goods on a large scale

assembly line a method of production in which a product moves through the factory while workers add parts to it

Technology and Inventions

Technology helps people find ways to make work easier, faster, and more efficient. **Technology** is the use of science for a purpose. An **inventor** uses technology to develop a new device or process, or solve a problem. Some of these changes are positive. For example, technology helps people build better bridges and roads. We can carry goods to people that live far away. But technology has also had negative effects. Many machines pollute the air, water, and soil.

Technology and Our Homes

Technology has also changed our homes. Technology is now part of everyday life. But some technology is old, such as a pair of scissors, which is a tool. This tool was invented long ago.

Technology makes it easier to do things in our homes. Calculators make it easier to solve hard math problems. Cellular phones make it easier to talk to other people. Dishwashers and microwave ovens make work in the kitchen easier and quicker. Refrigerators and freezers help us store food for a long time.

We use technology for entertainment too. Television and radio are the results of technology. You also use technology when you play a video game or a CD. CD technology led to the production of DVDs.

Technology has also changed how our homes look. Now, we build huge towers in which many people can live, in apartments.

Technology and Our Jobs

Technology has changed the way we work. Communities change when work changes. For example, manufacturing changed the way people work. **Manufacturing** is the production of many goods. In the early 1900s, cars had to be built one at a time. This was a slow process and cars were expensive.

Henry Ford used technology to solve this problem. He invented the **assembly line.** In an assembly line, workers add parts to a car as it moves through the factory. This new way of making cars was much faster. The price of cars went down. More people bought cars. This led to huge changes in society.

The assembly line is still used today. Now, robots and other machines are used to add parts. Robots are cheaper than people and make fewer mistakes. However, there is also a negative effect to using robots. People lose their jobs to machines.

© Pearson Education, Inc. 5

Lesson 1 Checkpoint

1. What are some positive and negative effects of technology?

_____

_____

_____

2. Give two examples of technology that you use in the home every day. What problems did these technologies solve?

_____

_____

_____

3. Give an example of an invention that has led to another invention.

_____

_____

4. How did the assembly line change society?

_____

_____

_____

Lesson 2: How has technology changed transportation?

Transportation Technology

Transportation is used to move people or things from place to place. Technology has changed our methods of transportation from the 1700s. Technology developed ships, trains, and planes and has made them faster and safer.

Steam engines were developed in the 1700s. These engines were used to power machines in factories and mines. At the same time, inventors worked to build steamboats with the steam engines. Steam engines made it possible for boats to move as easily up river as down river. In 1804, a steam engine was used to power a passenger train that carried iron and 70 people. This product of technology helped to change transportation.

In 1885, the safety bicycle was invented. It also replaced transportation by horse. This had a huge effect on society.

The first airplane flew in 1903. Planes began to change the way people and things moved. Early airplanes were used to deliver mail. Then planes were used in the military. People began to use planes to travel. Planes were able to carry people across oceans and countries.

Gas engines and electric motors continue to change transportation. Modern ships use diesel engines to generate power for the electric motors that make ships move. Electric motors are also used today on some cars and trains.

Technology May Bring Problems

Gas engines have had a positive effect on society. These engines are used in many different kinds of transportation, such as cars, taxis, ambulances, and tractors. Taxis help people move around in busy cities. Ambulances help people get to the hospital. Tractors help farmers grow food.

Gas engines have created new problems too. Gas engines cause air pollution. Gas engines can also lead to water pollution. Gasoline comes from crude oil. We get crude oil from the bottom of the sea. Sometimes, the oil spills back into the water and pollutes it.

Cars powered by gasoline not only pollute but create safety problems. Car engineers try to make safer cars. Seat belts are in every car. Airbags help protect people during accidents.

© Pearson Education, Inc. 5

Lesson 2 Checkpoint

1. Name two developments in transportation technology that changed the way people traveled after the mid-1800s.

   _____

   _____

2. What products of technology helped to replace transportation by horse?

   _____

   _____

3. What is one problem that has resulted from gasoline-powered cars?

   _____

   _____

4. **Sequence** Place the following inventions in the proper sequence in which they were developed: passenger train, steam engine, airplane, and the safety bicycle.

   _____

   _____

   _____

Lesson 3: How have computers changed society?

Vocabulary

microchip a small piece of a computer that contains microscopic circuits

World Wide Web a computer-based network of computers

Electronic Computers

Computer technology began in the 1930s. Early computers were very large and heavy and usually filled whole rooms. They weighed thousands of pounds.

Early computers were too large and too expensive to be practical. One of the most important inventions in computer technology was the microchip. A **microchip** is a small piece of a computer. It contains microscopic circuits. The microchip helped make computers less expensive, smaller, and able to process information faster.

In the 1980s, computer technology was used to solve another problem. A scientist wanted to easily communicate with other scientists. So he invented the World Wide Web. The **World Wide Web** is a computer-based network of computers. The Web was completed in 1990. Today, you can search for all kinds of information on the Web.

Being able to find so much information has created some problems. People use the web to spread misinformation throughout the computer network. Another problem is identity theft. Identity theft happens when someone uses another person's name and personal information to commit fraud or theft.

Computers for Science and Business

Today's computers can do very difficult work in seconds. But sometimes jobs are difficult even for a computer. Powerful supercomputers or computer networks can help to complete these jobs.

Computers can be used with other tools to produce better results. Telescopes, microscopes, cameras, and microphones can be used with computers. Computers can be used to focus telescopes. Microchips allow digital cameras to take and store pictures without using film. Microphones can be connected to computers allowing people to hear things they usually cannot hear.

Computers are helpful when a job needs to be done correctly. Computers are also used in dangerous situations. Computerized robots can do things humans cannot do. For example, robots can collect samples on Mars. This is just one way that computers make very difficult jobs possible.

Lesson 3 Checkpoint

1. What computer technology invention made computers smaller, faster, and inexpensive?

_____

2. What is the World Wide Web?

_____

_____

3. How did the invention of the microchip change computers?

_____

_____

_____

Lesson 4: What technology is used in space?

Vocabulary

space station a place where people can live and work in space for long periods of time

The Space Race

After World War II, there were strong political differences between the United States and the Soviet Union. The Space Race was a result of the competition between these countries to explore space. Many space missions were completed during this race.

Milestones in Space

This list shows some important events that happened during and after the Space Race:

- 1957: A Soviet satellite is the first to orbit space. The satellite is called *Sputnik 1.*
- 1957: A dog named Laika becomes the first animal in space, sent into orbit by the former Soviet Union.
- 1961: The Soviet Union sends the first man into space. His name is Yuri Gagarin.
- 1966: The Soviet Union is the first to land a probe on the Moon's surface.
- 1969: Two Americans land on the Moon. Neil Armstrong and Buzz Aldrin are the first people to walk on the Moon. The United States is considered to have won the Space Race.
- 1981: *The Space Shuttle Columbia* is sent into space. It is the first reusable spaceship.

- 1986: The Soviet Union builds the first permanent space station named *MIR.*
- 2000: The first crew arrives on the *International Space Station (ISS).* One American and two Russians make up this crew.
- 2003: China launches its first person into space.
- 2004: *SpaceShipOne,* the first privately owned spaceship, reaches space.

Space Station

A **space station** is a place where people can live and work in space for long periods of time. Many experiments cannot be done on a short space shuttle trip. People living in a space station can do these experiments. They can stay at a space station for months or years.

In 1998, the *International Space Station (ISS)* was put into space. It was built by the European Space Agency, the United States, Russia, Japan, Brazil, and Canada.

Solar panels supply power for the station's tools. These panels turn sunlight into electrical energy. Batteries store some of this power. The batteries are used when the station cannot receive sunlight.

New sections, or modules, are still being added to the *ISS*. It will be the about the size of a football field when it is completed and have a mass of almost 453.6 metric tons.

Lesson 4 Checkpoint

1. What two countries were involved in The Space Race?

   _____

2. Who was the first person in space?

   _____

3. Who were the first people to walk on the Moon?

   _____

   _____

4. **Sequence** Research four space events that are not mentioned in this lesson. Make a time line to sequence these events.